# Metaverse Investing Beginners Guide

*Buying Virtual Land, NFTs, VR, And*
*Other Digital Arts Of The Future*

Damon Berry

# Introduction

"Metaverse is the future." If you are interested in internet technologies, you have probably heard that phrase before. Is it true? Should you care? Both Mark Zuckerberg and Bill Gates have answered that question with a resounding yes. Facebook's Zuckerberg has even rebranded himself to fit the new territory. So indeed, the metaverse is the next big thing—what people who missed the "Web 2.0 train" have been waiting for.

The idea of a metaverse has been around for a while. The term was coined by Neal Stephenson in the 1992 novel Snow Crash. In the novel, protagonist Hiro meets a skateboarder who refers to herself as "Yours Truly." The two strike up a partnership and start conspiring against the government and mafia. Once the metaverse is fully realized, this scenario could easily be a Sunday afternoon activity for us.

Thankfully, technology is catching up to the idea, making the metaverse an increasingly important concept. Virtual reality (VR), Artificial intelligence (AI), and blockchains are all examples of pieces of the metaverse slowly coming together. Funding and R&D from big names will be one of the final pieces of the puzzle. It seems we may be on our way. As part of their Metaverse initiative, Microsoft is creating business tools. They aim to enable businesses to create virtual and augmented reality environments where employees can meet using its software products, such as Microsoft Teams. In the meantime, Facebook is working with Non-governmental organizations (NGOs) worldwide to keep the foundation of the metaverse ethically sound.

Now you might be thinking, "Isn't living through your avatar in a virtual world already a thing?" You're absolutely right. Second Life, for instance, is a classic example of a virtual world with its own culture and financial system. This is why it has come up in discussions about the metaverse. The metaverse we are discussing today, however, is a broader concept. The process involves entering cyberspace with VR glasses and fully interacting with the surroundings as if they were in person. In that case, Second Life would be part of the metaverse and not a metaverse in and of itself.

Mark Zuckerberg describes the metaverse as an embodied internet, which implies the metaverse will be an upgrade to the internet as we know it, perhaps going so far as to replace it. Tim

Sweeney, the founder of Epic Games, follows a similar approach. He says that he imagines the metaverse to be "a kind of online playground where users could join friends to play a multiplayer game like Epic's 'Fortnite' one moment, watch a movie via Netflix the next."

The tech giants clearly have a vision of the internet's future, and the metaverse is going to play a crucial role. It may not be at our doorstep just yet, but Web 3.0 is definitely around the corner, with technology advancing at a rapid pace. The metaverse is already home to a number of people working on content, selling virtual land, and more. Cryptocurrencies have become more popular than ever before, and are becoming a more respected investment tool. Consequently, the concept of making money from the metaverse is also becoming more prevalent.

In this book, we will dive deep into the metaverse. We will cover technology, philosophy, economics, and more, so you will be equipped with all the knowledge you need to take part in this revolution.

Now, without further ado, let's tackle the question of what exactly is the metaverse.

# What Is the Metaverse All About?

Imagine a world where you can virtually be present at a wedding in San Francisco while you're sipping a cup of coffee in Moscow? Or a society where interacting with people is not limited to just blurry video calls and glitchy computer service.

These are the things the metaverse, the next generation of the web, intends to do. But exactly, what is this metaverse? What sets it apart from the rest of the Internet?

A Metaverse is a place where you can interact with virtual items in real-time and with real-time information. In films and shows like Iron Man, Ready Player One, Upload, and The Feed, you've probably already seen this concept being put into practice.

The Metaverse consists of three distinct components. It is first and foremost a technology that allows digital content to be placed on top of the real-world environment. In a way, this is like augmented reality (AR). Using Pokémon Go as a simplistic example, this technology can be improved in future iterations of a metaverse. It's a mix of the digital and real-world stuff. It also uses a hardware gadget to make the natural environment interactive. Using digital material, users can manipulate and interact with media displayed online. The last point includes information on anything and everything in the real world (such as an area, a shop, or a product), along with information about the user (such as the user's timetable). This data will be gleaned through the Internet and machines trained to pick up on users' habits. There are many examples of devices learning from their users' daily behaviors, like Siri (iOS) and Alexa (Android) (on Amazon).

A user's experience is enhanced by obtaining real-time information instantly and virtually through the device into the physical space. At the same time, data is being collected and applied in the background.

To better grasp the Metaverse, one can extrapolate real-world traits to an entirely virtual setting. A metaverse environment will incorporate elements of the actual world into a virtual one. A virtual London or New York, for example, may provide digital representations of real-life streets and buildings to gamers playing in a virtual gaming environment. In a virtual Apple store, you may look through and purchase digital representations of Apple products that will be shipped to your home.

This would, in many ways, represent a continuation of what we currently know as traditional e-commerce. Companies may construct metaverse worlds that not only duplicate the real-life experience but also enhance it, thanks to advances in visual technology and design capability enabled by sophisticated gaming engines like Unreal or Unity. There may be no crowd outside the Manhattan Apple store's digital counterpart at launch time.

The concept of simulating real-world settings in a virtual one is nothing new. It has been going on for a long time with concepts like second life. On the other hand, contemporary online gaming settings have shifted the Metaverse from the old-school 3D block-based worlds of the turn of the century to new, ever-evolving creative ecosystems.

User-created content is the critical difference between the metaverses of the past and today. Playing online games like Fortnite, Roblox, and Minecraft has altered our perceptions of what it means to be "online." When parents wonder why their children spend so much time in these metaverse worlds, it's not because the games or items are well-designed.

Instead, they argue that the metaverses are so compelling and well-designed in and of themselves. People participate, create, and amuse each other rather than just sitting back and watching others. People are paid to make virtual goods in Minecraft, and entire mini-industries have sprung up around them. Fortnite is a virtual stage for real-world music performers to showcase their talents. Every year, tens of millions of people participate in activities that could only occur in the Metaverse.

## How Will the Metaverse Work?

To establish a connection with the Metaverse, one will almost certainly require the usage of a device. These goggles, a camera-equipped headmounted gadget, or other innovative inventions are all possibilities. While they aren't required to participate in the Metaverse, these gadgets may undoubtedly enhance the experience. Users will interact with virtual items in real life by "wearing" a device that integrates all of its components.

To put this idea into practice, imagine waking up every day, donning your metaverse goggles, and entering the Metaverse.

Think this is all just science fiction? No, not at all.

The Google Glass goggles were initially designed to be used for this purpose. You'll be able to observe and interact with virtual information as you walk down the street.

There is a possibility that you are walking to the railway station, and a virtual notification informs you of significant train delays. After that, you have the option of using a quicker route, such as public transportation or carpooling.

This is just a tentative example of how the Metaverse can work in real life. And if you still doubt it is happening, think again. The revolution has already begun.

Virtual items are presented in front of you, in the actual world, in real-time, and you can interact with them. Think of yourself as Tony Stark.

Using your artificial intelligence (AI) helper, you'll be able to find and see the information you're looking for in the actual world virtually. You can then view, click on, or otherwise interact with the things that appear.

Mobile technology has already made it possible for people to live in an enhanced reality, unnerving as it may sound. Your device is aware of your location and time. Since the Internet was created, integrating the real world with the virtual world has been an ongoing process. The Metaverse's primary function is to provide a means of distancing oneself from the realities of the real world. Adventures and alternate lives are possible in Fortnite for those who wish to do so. This escapist worldview has seen a substantial transformation in recent years with the inclusion of real-life components. Is watching a movie on Roblox something you'd like to do? You're playing Grand Theft Auto, and you'd want to buy some sneakers. On TikTok, you may watch a K-pop band's most recent live performance. As trade and engagement move online and into virtual worlds, the Metaverse is fueled by this virtual and real-life convergence. What are the commercial uses of the Metaverse, and who will reap the benefits? To put it another way, the introduction of the Metaverse will change our lives forever. Every industry has potential for metaverse applications.

The possibilities the Metaverse will unlock are endless, from consumer driven ones like retail to manufacturing and construction and beyond.

It is possible to make purchases in a flash. You won't even have to touch your smartphone to see a product when you see it in a store or on the Metaverse. Through a single account, customers may buy products and compare pricing. Due to improved connectivity, businesses will sell their products anywhere globally, regardless of where their retail locations may be.

Thanks to this new technology, businesses and celebrities will reach a far broader audience and collaborate more easily. In the future, customers will be able to communicate directly with brands. If employed correctly, this could have an excellent commercial influence. Brands and celebrities will see an increase in exposure. There may even be a market for virtual real estate in the Metaverse. Non-fungible tokens and other digital products and property will be given more attention in the future (NFTs). Because they aren't subject to wear and tear, items that can be traded are more valuable. Players may look forward to more immersive and interconnected game worlds in the future. A skin or item acquired in one game can be utilized in another game or swapped for a different item. As virtual cinema allows for private viewings with friends, the social experience will also shift. Many businesses, including journalism, social media, technology, and retail, will find new monetizing methods. At the same time, people will meet, work, and socialize more agreeably online in the future. Intellectual property will play a significant role when it comes to creative activity. Because of its greater accessibility, information, products, entertainment, and social experiences are likely to benefit consumers the most from the Metaverse. The technology market will be dominated by hardware and software enterprises. Providing hardware and software for the Metaverse is expected to rise significantly. Businesses will be able to build their virtual worlds. This means that more people will see and hear about brands and celebrities. As technology improves, so will the potential to provide customers with more relevant commercial offerings and experiences.

Law and rules in the Metaverse are still in flux. Therefore, legal guidance will also be required. As the virtual and real worlds merge, there is a tremendous demand for assistance in data protection, privacy, advertising rules, and ensuring that commercial firm intellectual property assets are secured. For years to come, attorneys and legislators will face the issue of making sure that real-world laws are appropriately translated into the virtual world. The Metaverse is being built by whom? The gaming industry is one of the best examples of how the Metaverse can be used in business today. We can see how the Metaverse can transform the way people interact with digital and real worlds through games like Fortnite and Roblox. As a result, many of the gaming industry's biggest names are also at the forefront of technological innovation and growth in this sector. Take the game Roblox, for instance. The gaming firm, which went public in March 2021, partially laid out its ambition for the company and the adoption of the Metaverse in its prospectus. For Roblox, a pervasive human co-experience platform is the aim, as computing power, high-bandwidth Internet connections, and human interface technologies continue to increase (and even build an economy based on its currency, Robux). Second Life's founders, Linden Labs, also developed their currency and had a bigger GDP than some small countries at one point.

In this situation, user experience is only one factor. Using the prefix "meta" (meaning beyond) and the stem "verse," the word "metaverse" is formed (meaning the universe). Critics believe that several critical features must exist for the Metaverse to fulfill its full potential, including:

Persistence

The ability to give live, synchronous experiences 3. Interoperability

4. Value creation.

Many stakeholders (individuals, commercial companies, and governments) are expected to be involved in the creation and operation of the Metaverse. This makes sense. Developing a community of stakeholders in the Metaverse, like the current Internet, is necessary for new technologies, businesses, services, content creators, standards and protocols, legislation, and more.

Microsoft's HoloLens augmented reality headset and Facebook's recent purchase of Oculus VR, as well as Unity's significant investment in digital twin technology, all point to the fact that many of the current technology industry giants, such as Microsoft, Facebook, and Unity, will almost certainly play a significant role in the development of the Metaverse.

In the future of the Metaverse, there's no consensus on how it will work, who will develop it, or who will "own" it (if anyone).

However, the broad consensus is that it will exist and no longer be considered a figment of our imaginations.

No matter what happens in the future, one thing is clear:

The Metaverse will expand incrementally over time as capabilities evolve and synergies are formed.

## Metaverse's Investment Areas

Metaverse's investment framework, at this stage, focuses on 4 core tracks of investment opportunities

1、Underlying architecture, such as blockchain, NFT, virtual currency.

2. Back-end infrastructure, such as e.g. 5G, GPU, cloud computing, AI+.

3, front-end devices, such as AR/VR, smart wearable devices.

4、Scene content, such as games, smart medical, UGC design, smart education, etc.

Metaverse itself will form a brand-new experience. In general, it may be a 3D Internet, so the most basic thing is to have a 3D display experience as the entrance. VR and AR devices will eventually become the entrance to the Metaverse, the next-generation Internet, or the infrastructure of hardware devices.

In the future, to interact with these virtual objects in the Metaverse, you may use "tools" including hands, handles and even eyeballs, etc. In the process of interaction, the algorithms currently used in VR will be used, including some extensions on the algorithm.

Metaverse in addition to the social level, more may form a new economic system or a new social system, so digital assets will also be an important part. In the process of digital asset formation, including the interaction and application of digital assets, strong interaction between VR and AR type algorithms and Metaverse digital assets has been formed. For example, in the virtual meeting, some virtual digital images of people, the interaction of these digital images, the capture or manipulation of movements, have begun to use interaction algorithms and technologies.

Metaverse returns to the industry chain structure and can summarize the innovation links into four areas: underlying architecture, back-end infrastructure, front-end devices and scene content. The following is an elaboration of each of the four key industry segments according to.

1: Underlying architecture, such as blockchain & NFT.

Metaverse is an immersive virtual world close to the real one, and it is crucial to build the corresponding economic system.

There is a core issue I would like to ask you to think about: the previous ordinary virtual worlds (online games, communities, etc.) have been treated as ordinary entertainment tools rather than real "parallel worlds", mainly because: the assets of such virtual worlds cannot circulate smoothly in reality, and even if players put all their efforts to become "winners" in the virtual world, most likely they cannot change their status in reality; the fate of players in such virtual worlds is not in their own hands, and once the operator closes the "world", all the assets and achievements of players will be zeroed out.

The emergence of blockchain will perfectly solve the above two points and allow Metaverse to complete the evolution of the underlying architecture, which is an industry segment currently neglected by the market: blockchain can create a fully functioning economic system in Metaverse that is linked to the real world, players' assets can smoothly connect with reality, blockchain is completely decentralized and not controlled by a single party, and players can continuously invest resources.

NFT is the only cryptocurrency token representing digital assets in the blockchain framework, and will be the economic cornerstone of the Metaverse in the future. NFT can be bought and sold in the same way as physical assets, ensuring effective corroboration of the underlying assets in the Metaverse.

Currently, NFT benefits from the DeFi ecosystem and the Metaverse scenario to achieve prosperous development - the market space is expected to be at the tens of billions of dollars in 21 years already. The NFT transaction space in 2021Q1 reached $2 billion (already more than 8 times of the full year 2020), which is about $2 billion, and the annualized processed annual transaction volume is projected to be $48 billion. If the Metaverse scenario continues to contribute 27% (refer to 2020) of this share, the Metaverse-NFT segment will have a space of at least $13 billion in 2021.

2: Back-end infrastructure, such as 5G, GPU, cloud, AI+, etc. In addition to frameworks and protocols, the underlying technical support also includes 5G, GPU, cloud computing, AI, arithmetic and network infrastructure covering hardware and software.

Deduced from AV/VR, where there are two technical paths of stand-alone intelligence and net-linked cloud control. The former mainly focuses on the near-eye display, perceptual interaction and other fields, and the latter focuses on the streaming service service after the content is put on the cloud. It is judged that in the future Metaverse framework, the two will be organically integrated on the basis of 5G infrastructure, and AI + cloud resonance triggers industrial leap.

In terms of space, there are too many technology intersections, grasping the big one and focusing on AI+. Based on two aspects of data (the overall panAI space and the Metaverse-like scenario represented by AR/VR), the Metaverse-related AI+ technology support industry scale line strategy calculations: about 740 billion yuan of pan-AI industry space in 2021 will breed 40.7 billion yuan of Metaverse business space.

3: Front-end devices, such as AR/VR, wearable, etc. In terms of front-end devices, AR/VR and smart wearable devices are the basis for continuous and stable access to the Metaverse and immersive experience for users. From the perspective of the equipment industry chain: the core hardware links involve sensors, displays, processors, optical devices, etc.

From the industrial space, the overall value space of AR/VR virtual terminal equipment will reach 480 billion yuan by 2024, and the output value scale will be divided into two by AR/VR devices. It is judged that the market space of VR devices will be about 65 billion yuan in 2021, and the market space of AR devices will be about 50 billion yuan, that is, the market space of Metaverse key device side will be about 115 billion yuan. Meanwhile, it is expected that this space will rise to 480 billion yuan in 2024, and the compound annual growth rate will reach 54% according to the estimation above.

4: Scene content, such as games, industry, medical, education, etc.

Basic application stage: focused on games, short videos and other fields, with more limited content and a single interaction mode. Extended application stage: applied to all kinds of panoramic scenes, and to education, marketing, training, medical, industrial processing, architectural design and other scenes. Application ecological stage: eventually, Metaverse panoramic social will become one of the ultimate application forms of virtual reality.

The content side is the largest: In terms of business model, industry chain manufacturers can obtain income through channels such as sharing, commission, copyright fee and advertising fee. From the perspective of customer base, the content side will gradually penetrate from industry-level market to consumer-level market.

# Concepts of the Metaverse

During your research about the metaverse, you may come across terms with which you are unfamiliar. You should not let that prevent you from exploring this revolutionary technology. Let's discuss key concepts of the metaverse in a way that will help you get a better sense of what it all means.

<u>Blockchain</u>

IBM defines blockchain as a shared, immutable ledger that facilitates the process of recording transactions and tracking assets in a business network. That sounds a bit confusing, doesn't it? Let's make it simple.

Imagine a circle. The circle is filled with information. This information can be anything from contracts to shopping lists. When this information gets an update, another circle appears and connects itself to the first chain. Eventually, these circles form a chain, and the term blockchain is born. Each block is connected to every other block chronologically, and the chain goes on as long as it needs to.

Putting it this way, you might immediately think of old accounting books, and you would be absolutely correct. A blockchain is nothing more than a digital ledger. Any type of data can be recorded on a blockchain. What sets blockchains apart from the good old Excel sheet is security. Blockchains are nearly impossible to cheat or hack. But how? One word: decentralization.

Traditional ledgers use databases. The internet runs on databases, which have existed for decades. The problem with databases is that they use what's called 'CRUD.' CRUD stands for create, read, update, and delete. In other words, you can enter a database, examine data, make the necessary changes, or delete information. As a result, security risks arise since you aren't the only one capable of doing all those things. Third parties, hackers, and rogue administrators are all capable of changing or erasing your data.

This is why blockchain technology is absolutely revolutionary. Blockchains use a decentralized ledger. It is hosted on different computers, also known as nodes. This allows blockchain to support immutability. The moment data is written, it cannot be changed or erased, significantly minimizing the risk of third parties interfering.

Immutability offers more than just security. The immutability of blockchains makes them the most transparent and trustworthy ledgers out there. Blockchains have two functions: read and write. Which means you can retrieve information and add it to it. Databases, on the other hand, can be made public but can't be verified by individuals. Blockchains solve this issue, which is why cryptocurrencies like Bitcoin prefer using them.

Using a blockchain depends on your individual needs. Some blockchains are public, but there are also private options. You can choose to use a "permission system" that limits viewing to specific users. Each method has pros and cons regarding usage and security, but there is no doubt that blockchains are the best technology currently available.

The metaverse era will be based on decentralized currencies. We will discuss blockchain's role in cryptocurrencies in a moment. The bottom line is if you are interested in becoming a part of the metaverse, the blockchain is something with which you need to get familiar. Unless you do so, you will be vulnerable to market fluctuations, which are notoriously volatile in decentralized currencies.

<u>Cryptocurrency</u>

Since Bitcoin started making teenage millionaires, cryptocurrencies have become the talk of the town. There are a lot of questions about crypto currencies. Why do their values fluctuate so much? What makes them valuable in the first place? Can they be trusted? Is it real money? Should you invest in it? All of those questions have simple answers, and they all have to do with, you guessed it, decentralization.

In order to understand why cryptocurrencies are so successful, we must first learn how traditional currencies work. The distribution of money as we know it is controlled by central banks. A central bank's primary job is to control money circulation. They can do this by printing more banknotes, changing interest rates, setting reserve requirements, and so on.

It is a simple economic principle. If there is a scarcity of a commodity, the value goes up. If it is abundant, the value goes down. In order to stabilize the value of a currency and prevent inflation, central banks tweak the distribution on a regular basis.

This is not the case with cryptocurrency. You see, fiat money has no real value, it only has attributed value since the governments declare it legal tender, essentially making it debt. Most cryptocurrencies are finite. Bitcoin, for example, has a limited supply of 21 million, making it more valuable than gold. Consequently, its value is determined by its efficiency as a trade medium.

Bitcoins are not printed by central banks, so you might wonder how they get into circulation. That is where 'mining' comes in. In order to mine, sophisticated computing hardware is needed to solve complex mathematical problems. A cryptocurrency's value and availability depend heavily on this. That is why the cryptocurrency market will always be prone to volatility. For instance, there are currently about 18 million Bitcoins on the market. However, several millions of Bitcoins are lost in transactions. Since blockchains cannot be updated, only added, this will prove to be true for other virtual currencies in the future.

Understanding this aspect of cryptocurrencies is essential to generating income from them.

In the metaverse era, we can expect virtual and digital currencies to become even more significant. In the future, metaverses are expected to have their own currency or use one that is already available. Knowledge of virtual currency will prove to be useful to your business or the investment you intend to make. It makes or breaks you if you know how a coin's mining operation, blockchain, and developers work. Take the time to become familiar with different types of currencies, and remember that great opportunities await those who can recognize them.

<u>Smart Contracts</u>

IBM defines smart contracts as programs stored on a blockchain that run when predetermined conditions are met. Put simply, they really are 'smart' contracts. Your contract is sealed on a blockchain instead of a regular safe, and it will only be deemed valid once your arrangement is fulfilled.

Furthermore, they are fully automated. That means all parties who signed the contract will be aware of the outcome immediately. Through this technology, there is no need for third-party involvement or commissions. Smart contracts essentially make intermediaries redundant.

Smart contracts were first envisioned by American computer scientist Nick Szabo in 1994. He is considered to be one of the forefathers of decentralized currency. Szabo envisioned a virtual currency called Bit Gold in 1998, 10 years before Bitcoin was introduced. Some speculate that Szabo is the actual inventor of Bitcoin and used Satoshi Nakamoto as an alias. His idea was to further point of sale (POS) devices into the digital space. Therefore, he proposed a software protocol that included contract terms, called smart contracts today.

One of the most exciting aspects of smart contracts is their ability to automate workflow. In essence, you can specify the timeline and conditions of the project, and the contract will update itself if a condition is fulfilled. Businesses and managers will save a lot of time on meetings, conference calls, and expensive business trips.

Smart contracts are one of the features of Web 3.0 already in use. They can be used for a number of purposes, including but not limited to releasing funds to the appropriate parties, registering a vehicle, sending notifications, or issuing tickets. It is not hard to imagine that they will play an important role in contractual law and our daily lives.

Smart contracts can be developed by a programmer. However, as they become more mainstream, companies utilizing blockchain technology provide templates, web interfaces, and other online tools to make structuring smart contracts easier.

Smart contracts provide immediate execution, which prevents time loss and paperwork. Since the contract is between two anonymous parties and third parties aren't involved, the relationship between the partners is completely transparent. Blockchains, where the smart contracts are stored, are heavily encrypted, making smart contracts one of the most secure ways to conduct business. Finally, they are free from any third-party fees. These advantages will make future contracts a lot smarter.

<u>NFTs</u>

You might have seen on the news, GIF images or pixel art being sold for millions of dollars through a system called NFT. You might be wondering what makes a piece of digital art so valuable. What's even more confusing is that oftentimes these artworks are quite simple, and to the average eye, they look like they would hold no real value. Actually, NFTs are not complicated at all. Let's look at it from an artist's perspective.

Say you have a friend who's an artist, let's call him Gary. As an artist, Gary wants his art to be recognized by the masses. But he is also worried about copyrights. He is not wrong to be concerned. In the digital era, it's incredibly hard to track whether your art is being used legitimately or not. People copy paste images all the time. For all Gary knows, his designs are being sold on t-shirts in a remote part of the world. There is no sustainable way to track it. That's where NFTs come in.

The term NFT stands for "non-fungible token." It is a digital signature that cannot be changed. When Gary creates an NFT for his digital art, he does two things: First, he creates non-fungible ownership of his art. This part of an NFT works just like how a normal royalty would. By putting an NFT on his art, Gary makes sure he makes a royalty each time the item is sold. What sets apart NFTs from traditional royalty is the fact that they can be traded.

If Gary decides to sell his royalties, he can do so in a few minutes by changing his non-fungible token for cash, cryptocurrency, or another NFT. Gary's ownership is easily verified through his

NFT because it is being held in a blockchain. Remember that blockchains don't allow users to change data, only add to it. This allows Gary to verify his ownership over his art any time he wants.

Artists need NFTs for sure, but there is a bigger picture. NFTs will be the future of digital ownership. As everything becomes digitized, we need ownership protection systems like NFTs more than ever. In the short term, NFTs are expected to expand into fields including music, sports, and gaming, as well as other industries in the long-term. They are well on their way to becoming a digital property standard, making them an excellent investment opportunity.

<u>Artificial Intelligence</u>

Simply put, artificial intelligence (AI) is the intelligence demonstrated by machines. The purpose of artificial intelligence is to simulate the human brain and provide cognitive functions such as decision-making. Artificial intelligence has created many debates over the decades about whether or not it can take over human tasks. Some believe artificial intelligence is simply there to help humanity, while others argue allowing machines to think for themselves could be catastrophic. We will go into some detail about this debate without getting bogged down in technological jargon. However, it will be to your advantage to learn more about artificial intelligence, as the outcome of this debate will determine what the metaverse will look like.

The debate goes all the way back to the 1950s. Known as the father of computer science, Alan Turing advocated a humanistic approach. In his opinion, artificial intelligence had to be systems that think and act like humans. He created the famous Turing Test, which uses human interrogators to distinguish between human and computer responses. The test has been criticized a lot since then, but Alan Turing cracked the Enigma code and helped end World War II, so his opinions are not easily dismissed.

The other side of the debate follows a more pragmatic approach. It is championed by Stuart Russell and Peter Norvig, the authors of the seminal book *Artificial Intelligence: A Modern Approach*. They argued for an ideal approach over a human approach in which artificial intelligence would think and act rationally instead of intuitively like a human.

Metaverse will rely heavily on artificial intelligence and machine learning. Without them, devices intended to make our lives easier will not be available. Whether those devices will think like us and provide us with what they think we want is different from the machines making rational choices for us. Although artificial intelligence as a concept has existed for quite some time, its implementation to the end-user is relatively new. As technology continues to develop, we will have access to various forms of artificial intelligence. There will certainly be some interesting decisions made by tech giants, and how government regulations will react to it remains to be seen.

<u>Augmented Reality</u>

Augmented reality (AR) and virtual reality (VR) are often confused or used interchangeably. These are two separate concepts, and you need to learn how to differentiate them while conducting your metaverse research. Augmented reality adds digital elements to a real-life environment, like TikTok filters. Virtual reality, on the other hand, consists of a completely artificial environment that exists outside the real world. We will talk about virtual reality in a moment, but first, let's dive deeper into augmented reality.

We can expect to see augmented reality more in the early stages of Web 3.0. While it is not an easy technology to develop, making it accessible to the general public is much easier. Because of this, companies are coming up with augmented reality features first so they can get a foothold, while their virtual reality projects are still in development. Furthermore, augmented reality is simply cool and fun. Billions of people use augmented reality in the workplace, on social media, and for entertainment, while entirely disconnecting from the real world is scary to many.

But there is a sweet spot for this in the metaverse called mixed reality (MR). The mixed reality is where virtual reality and augmented reality meet to enhance the user experience. Together, all this process is referred to as extended reality (XR) and it will be a crucial aspect of the metaverse. Mark Zuckerberg and like-minded entrepreneurs advocate for a metaverse that will cut us from reality and into a new one. In their vision, augmented reality and virtual reality work hand in hand as extended reality to push the boundaries of reality as we know it.

Others like John Hanke of Google advocate for a different approach. They believe the real metaverse will rely heavily on augmented reality. This is similar to what they envision with Pokemon Go. Imagine taking a stroll in your city with augmented reality glasses. Upon reaching a historical building or statue, the glass could then display a convincing 3D animation of historic events to transport you back in time. Perhaps you are in an art district, in which case the glass could display a digital exhibition without having to go inside a museum.

The fact is virtual reality and augmented reality are inextricably linked.

Basically, augmented reality gives the illusion of artificial objects in the real world, while virtual reality gives the illusion of inhabiting an artificial environment. Regardless of the debates, the fact remains. Augmented reality is a great technology, and we will see more of it.

<u>Virtual Reality</u>

Virtual reality (VR) is a computer technology used for creating simulated environments. Therefore, virtual reality is absolutely crucial to the metaverse as it is one of the main characteristics that will distinguish Web 2.0 from Web 3.0. In Web 2.0, the user interface is a primary component. We interact with the user interface using a mouse or touchpad on our computers and clicking on a screen on our smartphones. In virtual reality, however, we will interact with the environment more naturally by using a head-mounted display (HMD). The headset and glasses will simulate the real world with realistic 3D environments and sounds.

The entertainment aspect of virtual reality will be a game-changer, but there are other important implementations as well. Virtual reality is expected to change many industries. Medical students can perform simulated surgery on realistic patients to gain experience. Soldiers can train in tough war games without destroying the environment or spending tax dollars on real equipment. Athletes can continue training when injured without compromising their cognitive performance. This technology is likely to reduce costs and improve efficiency in almost every industry.

Metaverse experiences will be highly customized by virtual reality. However, it will be a while for virtual reality to be a mainstream activity. Even with glasses and headsets available, virtual reality still needs a significant amount of computing power to operate properly. Without it, it is prone to problems like image latency and display refresh frequency. Luckily, high-performance processors are becoming more affordable and accessible to the majority of us, so we can expect to see a lot more virtual reality in the near future.

<u>Virtual Land</u>

Are you wondering who owns the metaverse? Well, you do! People who create metaverses do not intend to hold the land for themselves. Why would they? It is, after all, land, and land can be rented out or sold. Perhaps you think it is ridiculous if not borderline crazy to pay for digital land. Republic Realm, a virtual real estate developer, purchased a piece of property in The Sandbox for $4.3 million, and they would like to disagree with you. Another example is a Twitter user who goes by the name Flying Falcon. They announced making a $1.5 million purchase in the AxieInfinity metaverse, claiming it will be the "Hamptons of the metaverse." It is clear that virtual land is on the radar of both individual investors and investment groups alike. But what makes virtual land so alluring and expensive?

What makes virtual land expensive is the building and maintenance costs associated with it. It takes a lot of servers, processing, and electric power to build and maintain a metaverse. As such, they are valuable pieces of digital assets. It is actually smart on the creator's part to sell the land instead of keeping it as an investment themselves. Additionally, by selling the land, they create an investor user base that will bring in more end users into the metaverse. This is a great help with keeping their customer acquisition costs low.

Although virtual land may be a great investment, the risks associated with it are still very high. In the same vein, if you are a high-risk/high-reward investor, this is a very lucrative investment opportunity. Cryptocurrency will be spent on your virtual land and your investment will net great returns as long as that currency rises. Be sure to examine the currency and blockchain carefully before making a virtual land purchase. If you think they have the right infrastructure, buy early for the highest possible return on investment.

# NFT Video Gaming

There is a lot of precedent for what the metaverse will look like in the realm of video games.

Gaming in the future might look and feel different. Still, at its foundation, it's likely to be similar to how players currently immerse themselves in a game's world and atmosphere. So, what will be different? The main difference is in monetization.

So, what will be different? The NFTs, in the metaverse, will be applied to everything that can be tokenized, including in-game assets.

The gaming sector is a prime target for the "endowment effect" of NFTs.

Game creators and publishers have long leveraged gamers' desire to acquire extra powers, features, and assets as a means of selling their games. It's a historically effective strategy.

However, players may get frustrated when they realize their "purchases" only last as long as they keep playing the game they've "purchased" it in.

Your dazzling virtual objects disappear when you start a new game. NFTs are considered a solution to "address" the problem of players believing they "own" their in-game assets by making them sellable to others and transferable from one game to another.

Tokenized game asset exchanges are available. The misconception that a digital asset may be converted into a traded good using NFTs must be dispelled. Whether or not an in-game asset can be sold to another player depends on whether the game publisher supports the idea of tradability and has put in place the required infrastructure in-game to support it.

In theory, a games publisher that allows in-game asset trade may not need to tokenize its assets on the blockchain to do so.

Just because something is more complicated doesn't mean it's necessarily better. In addition, game publishers would be able to commission each sale and continue to monetize their assets, albeit from a new aspect, if they controlled their in-game marketplaces.

This in-game solution would significantly align with what happens when players "buy" and "sell" in-game assets.

In-game assets cannot be sold independently from their intellectual property, as stated in the NFTs section, and game publishers are not in the business of selling their intellectual property lightly.

The in-game assets also include licenses, not sales, as we said when talking about non-financial transactions in art. As explained in the game's terms and conditions, they grant you access to the object for a specific period and within a particular context.

Will in-game assets never be traded on NFT marketplaces because of this decision?

Probably not. NFT games are currently generating a lot of hype. Still, caution is advised because licenses are more difficult to sell than property rights.

This could lead to the demise of NFT games due to a lack of value.

A prime example of items that will eventually be traded in the Metaverse gaming NFT marketplace is portable game assets.

The ability to use your leveled-up rare sword, for example, from one game to the next, would be fantastic.

<u>Can NFTs Make This a Reality?</u>

Again, there's more to this story than meets the eye. Unlike in the real world, you can't easily pack up your blade and go on a trip with it. If the sword isn't in your host game, good luck using it to sever the heads of your foes. What's the point of creating a "foreign" word if the publisher already has some perfectly good ones available for you to use within their game world? You can't utilize a sword made for a video game in any other capacity. Nothing is more assured until the two corporations agree to make portability possible. There is little doubt that firms will take notice of the demand from gamers is strong enough. However, we believe that in game assets (including characters) will only be transferred between games developed by the same company for the foreseeable future. It's important to remember that most gamers don't give a hoot about the legal ramifications of their purchases if they can have a fun time playing the game.

According to the endowment effect, there will undoubtedly be a widening gap between what games are composed of and what people believe they are.

This is a precondition for the metaverse to be a viable alternative to the real world; it should closely resemble it.

The metaverse gaming prospect relies heavily on advanced technology.

Fortunately, corporations do not have to spend as much money on infrastructure.

Processor and graphics technology advancements have been spurred on for years by a booming video game sector. Today, we are getting ever closer to photorealistic gaming experiences. It is just a matter of time before intellectual property and licensing issues take center stage in the gaming industry. There is no way around the inherent limits of that approach when applied to a notion of interoperability imposed by video games as a prototype for the metaverse.

Problems with NFT and related tokenization are more manageable than those connected to the metaverse's underlying infrastructure, in specific ways at least. Why should we assume that the metaverse would look like a single planet where everyone on it can connect and interact in all of these ways: love, hate, fight, reconcile, exploit, and heal?

Multiple metaverses, segregated at the very least by platform configurations but maybe also by content, genres, and publishing rights, are significantly more likely due to the intellectual property and the accompanying license.

The financial motive that has fueled technological growth is the construction of barriers between competing worlds. Metaverse's paradigm as a video game hints at the limitations built into the infrastructure that would create the virtual world. A metaverse that spans jurisdictions and platforms may exist. Still, it will be shattered by intellectual property laws, antitrust laws, privacy regulations, and the capitalistic ethos that has driven the video game industry for decades. When it comes to power, the metaverse's infrastructure will once again raise concerns about the amount of energy needed to run the CPUs and graphics chips.

Video games and the companies building the infrastructure that will support future generations of games and perhaps even a metaverse can serve as helpful guides. Sustainability and energy saving will be essential differentiators for organizations vying for market share in video games and platforms. People who want to make video games more immersive will need to be environmentally responsible (both in terms of energy usage and sustainable construction materials).

Game developers must consider green alternatives instead of simply creating more massive and voracious appetites for the earth's resources.

This is especially important since public opinion appears to be shifting toward a shared goal of preserving our planet.

Metaverse Gaming and Laws

Modesty has its bounds when it comes to the nature of human beings. Online video games and the platforms that host and market them teach us another important lesson: if left unchecked, they may degrade into hazardous environments.

Already countries around the globe are beginning to regulate the Metaverse gaming system.

For example, the EU Directive 2010/13/EU amendments seek to align nonlinear service regulation with linear TV restrictions to protect minors and harmful content and include specific video-sharing platforms (VSP) requirements to protect minors from harmful content.

Other European countries are also beginning to step up their regulation of the web.

Children (under 18) are the focus of the new ICO Age-Appropriate Design Code in the United Kingdom, which went into effect in September 2021.

The code recommends certain default settings for services that are likely to attract children, including considering children's best interests when designing any data processing in services.

A new German law, the Federal Protection of Young Persons Act (Jugendschutzgesetz - JuSchG), which took effect on May 1, 2021, aims to protect children and young people from harm caused by media consumption and ensure that media is only distributed or made available following the applicable age classification.

The various types of media and other publications that fall into this category include immoral and violent content; the detailed presentation of violent acts, murder, and massacre; and the recommendation of "the law of the jungle" to obtain 'justice.'

The French government has also enacted several laws that regulate online behavior.

One stands out: the pending French audiovisual reform draft law, which would combine the Conseil Supérieur de l'Audiovisuel (CSA) and the Haute Autorité pour la Diffusion des Oeuvres et la Protection des Droits sur Internet (HADOPI) into a single entity.

Among the many new powers that would be granted to this new "superregulator," known as the Audiovisual and Digital Communication Regulatory Authority (ARCOM), would be the ability to regulate online platforms and combat harmful content on the Internet, and improve the fight against piracy.

It is uncertain if governments can successfully control and promote the moderation they now do in video games in the metaverse. Yet, it is possible in the real world.

If the idea of "platform" becomes nebulous, what liability might be imposed on a developer that does not implement anti-online harm moderation requirements on their platforms?

Would the regulators be required to interact with the public in the virtual world, like Agent Smith in The Matrix?

These issues will unfold in the coming years as the metaverse is continually being developed. All enthusiastic fans and loyalists of the concept can do is wait.

## Music and Metaverse

When compared to other industries, the music sector has always, historically speaking, been the first to react to any new internet invention.

Everyone is aware that the music industry was significantly disrupted and transformed beyond recognition in the early days of internet development.

As a result of the COVID-19 epidemic, the music industry, mainly performing artists, has been forced to innovate and find new ways to connect with their audiences.

As a result, they began to perform on the Internet.

To be fair, online streaming is not a new concept. Bands like the Rolling Stones were doing it as early as 1995. Streaming music is, in fact, the entire market model of companies like Spotify.

However, music consumption in the metaverse differs significantly from typical "vanilla" live streaming, or even subscription streaming, in several important ways.

Listed below are the differences.

The Ability to Create, Or to Perform In, A Virtual Venue

Using an avatar or other visual representation of the artist, sometimes mixed with an authentic video representation of the artist.

New production capabilities, such as manipulating the virtual environment and combining digital visual production with the artist's musical production

The Ability to Interact with The Audience In Realtime

The performance by Travis Scott on Fortnite was likely the most striking and commercially successful example of this revolutionary musical art form in recent years.

The performance by Travis Scott on Fortnite was likely the most striking and commercially successful example of this revolutionary musical art form in recent years.

This event generated a significant amount of attention and interest for this event.

Aside from virtual events and NFTs, another metaverse trend that has impacted the music industry is the emergence of virtual "artists."

The thought of listening to a virtual artist, who is made by artificial intelligence and does not have a real personality, may be repulsive to many serious music enthusiasts.

Despite this, there is no disputing that such musicians are gaining significant traction among young people who grew up with the Internet. The rapper FN Meka, who has been described as a "robot rapper known for his flamboyant style and Hypebeast aesthetics," is an excellent illustration.

While this may appear to be a frivolous, slightly futuristic bit of entertainment, it is built on a foundation of serious commercial possibilities. While writing this book, the virtual rapper has over 9 million followers on the TikTok video-sharing app.

Comparatively, Chance the Rapper, who is sometimes referred to as "one of the new crops of superstar rappers," had less than 2 million TikTok followers when writing this book.

These two incidents beg the question:

Is The Metaverse a Source of Opportunity Or A Source Of Danger For Music?

Both opportunities and threats for the music industry can arise from the metaverse, as demonstrated by the two cases presented above. Artistic careers are at risk if they rely on outdated methods that are no longer relevant in today's world of cutting-edge production and consumption methods and consumer experiences. For example, suppose you only possess the rights and monetize through subscription streaming channels. In that case, you won't be making enough money to justify your investment in these methods. They'll quickly become commoditized and automated.

Business opportunities are virtually limitless for those willing to push the boundaries and use all available technology to interact and create. Compared to online metaverse performances, even the most extensive arena tours cannot handle anything near the instantaneous, one-time global crowds the artist can attract to a live online metaverse performance.

The COVID-19 pandemic, which caused the entire world to shift to the Internet for entertainment, has demonstrated to the music industry that ticketed, well-produced, and compelling live streaming will be around for the foreseeable future. It is conceivable that the most significant concerts and festivals that take place in the actual world will in the future have an online component that is more committed, sleek, and transactional. Because of this, the metaverse will continue to exist in music for the foreseeable future.

Because of this, the metaverse will continue to exist in music for the foreseeable future.

<u>What Are the Legal Ramifications of Music Being Played In The Metaverse?</u>

When music is generated, played, streamed, and exploited online, rights clearances are the most important consideration, as they are in all aspects of the music industry. Most of the standard legal and licensing regulations for online exploitation apply in the metaverse, with some exceptions. However, music performance and exploitation in new, closed, or even open online environments add another potential layer of complexity to an already complex chain of rights in the music licensing process.

For example, a digital music service provider (such as Spotify) may promote and organize a live-streamed concert on a worldwide games console platform (such as the Sony PlayStation).

This concert could occur during the tournament's intermission being held and marketed by a leading games publisher (such as Electronic Arts) who might be collaborating with a well-known brand during the interval of the event (e.g., Adidas).

Those interested in attending would need to be registered users of the gaming platform and have acquired entrance tickets to the eSports competition. Although the live-streamed concert would be available to a restricted number of superfans who joined a prize drawing by purchasing an original NFT token issued by the headline performing artist, the performance would only be open to the general public (for example, Drake).

Top-level prizes may include attendance at the live virtual event and an actual piece of digital goods.

Runners-up would still be able to watch the concert on-demand later, even though they'd be missing out on the thrill of a live show. The network of contractual responsibilities to negotiate and the rights-clearance concerns to consider, as illustrated by the example above, are not unlike the issues that lawyers may encounter in the real world when dealing with clients. The halftime show for the NFL Super Bowl is well-known in the music industry for being a highly prestigious but demanding production and clearance exercise that requires much planning and coordination. However, in many ways, the amount of complexity associated with clearing music for the metaverse can be substantially higher than the level of complexity associated with clearing music for the physical world.

Therefore, anyone wishing to use another's music in the metaverse must ensure that the terms under which they receive a license are compatible with where it is being utilized. While this appears to be straightforward in concept, a genuinely global virtual environment is governed in various ways depending on the legal jurisdiction. Censorship and content standards impacting a live performance by a Top 10 rap artist in the United States will be drastically different from those affecting a similar performance in, for example, Indonesia, Dubai, or Hong Kong. The political beliefs of artists are frequently expressed onstage.

These situations are more manageable in real life. Still, they are the stuff of nightmares for the legal compliance teams at large platforms, frequently tasked with maintaining positive relationships with local governments worldwide.

<u>Who Is Responsible for Clearing The Permissions?</u>

It may be claimed that customers are accustomed to the platforms themselves covering music licensing, at least when it comes to live performances or engagement with the public in the media. Twitch, Facebook, YouTube, TikTok, and PlayStation are online services that benefit from blanket agreements with music rights owners, collection organizations, and other online services.

At the very least, consumers can feel more confident about using music in the context they are operating, even though such sites' terms of service state unequivocally that music licensing falls solely upon the uploader. However, when music can be made, shared, and enjoyed in a real-time gaming metaverse or social setting, the situation becomes more complex and complicated.

By just establishing a meme, any user can now instantaneously control, tweak, and produce a whole new musical work that has the potential to go viral. These tools are publicly available and have the potential to cause widespread havoc.

The video-sharing app TikTok is unquestionably an essential platform for discovering and promoting new music at writing. Still, the users define whether a song will be successful more than ever. Because of the viral capacity of user-generated mashups and multiple synchronizations, lawyers who advise artists, labels, publishers, and even platforms themselves have an almost limitless number of opportunities for innovative licensing solutions, contentious disputes, and profitable transactional opportunities.

While the platform will be accountable for making reasonable attempts to get licenses for content posted by users, it will not be held liable for licensing copyrights in content brought to a platform by commercial operators (to put it bluntly). Suppose we apply this to the world of music. In that case, it instantly raises the question of whether a musician qualifies as a "professional user."

Artists as disparate as Ava Max, BTS, Marshmello, and Kaskade have performed through graphic representations in online gaming environments. At the same time, cutting-edge virtual reality services such as MelodyVR (now rebranded as the next generation "Napster") and Facebook's Oculus allow users to watch real-life concerts take place in a virtual reality format in real-time.

While there is no "one size fits all" method to securing rights for these types of events, there are several factors to consider:

The person who is performing

The legal framework under which the artist's recording and ancillary rights are controlled; the songs or works will be included in the performance.

It is essential to understand the following:

- Production components that are included (for example, choreography, which was previously the domain of only the most diligent of production rights clearance professionals, can now be a total minefield in the metaverse environment)

- The virtual engine that powers or underpins the production.

This includes the creative contributions of digital artists and other virtual participants.

Making Music in The Metaverse

Making new music in the metaverse will be a rewarding experience.

It goes without saying that if people begin to reside in the metaverse, project their image, and spend their time there, the next logical step for them is to transition from the real-world recording studio to the virtual creative environment. There are numerous examples of this already taking place in the world. A wide variety of virtual reality headsets and controllers that allow users to interact with graphical interfaces that simulate musical instruments are currently available. The air guitar transforms into a real guitar - Rock Band VR is on the horizon.

In this digital age, it is now feasible to form your band online and convert yourself from a balding, middle-aged "dad bod" into a lavishly coiffured, tanned, lithe rock hero who lives out your fantasy of playing guitar in front of large crowds. On a more practical level, metaverse environments such as Minecraft, Roblox, and Fortnite incorporate song codes, instruments, and recording facilities and controls for manipulating music, allowing players to express themselves musically. While the vast majority of this activity will result in original copyright that has little or no monetary worth, users have countless opportunities to infringe or encroach on well-known unknowingly, commercial music or assets, which could result in legal action.

Do you want to listen to some Frank Sinatra crooners in an electric jazz modern remix with your virtual buddies in the metaverse?

It's not a problem.

Of course, as the mix of innovative technology, people, and connection progresses, the complexity of the legal challenges also increases. Music is already one of the most convoluted, complex, and divergent aspects of entertainment law, and this is only the beginning. The prevalence and expansion of music in the metaverse indeed present new challenges. Still, it also offers enormous opportunities for lawyers to innovate and assist their clients – not only in navigating through the existing frameworks but also in developing new models and methods of exploitation of copyrights that contribute to the creation of incremental revenues and value for the industry, as well as for the platforms that invest in the metaverse itself.

# All About Artificial Intelligence

In recent years, artificial intelligence (AI) programs have gained the ability to behave intelligently and make music, art, and other forms of original creative output.

For $432,500, Christie's auctioned a portrait of Edmond de Belamy made by an artificial intelligence system three years ago.

SONY CSL Research Lab has also developed an artificial intelligence system called Flow Machines.

This AI program can compose new music based on anything from the Beatles to Bach, among other things. The Metaverse, whether it's an extension of the real world or any number of computer-generated worlds, is bound to include an overlying layer of unfathomably vast amounts of "data."

As a feature of that data, a person or entity creating and controlling an environment known as "the metaverse" will generate and disseminate that data.

Nevertheless, unlike the physical world, the Metaverse is wholly artificial. If a digital tree or cloud does not "belong" to its creator in the Metaverse, it will not exist in the Metaverse. We may anticipate that practically everything in the Metaverse, from the appearance of our avatars to the clothing we wear and the vehicles we drive, will be the intellectual property of someone. Artificial intelligence (AI) uses machine learning technologies to study, digest, and analyze massive amounts of data to develop rules of application, which are referred to as algorithms. The examination of fresh data sources and the observation of its own data output allow machine learning software to improve itself after it has been "trained continuously." A new branch of artificial intelligence has emerged in recent years, encompassing computing systems that try to emulate the function of the human brain in evaluating and processing information. These systems are referred to as artificial neural networks. They also include coupling computer networks in generative adversarial networks, in which the computers learn from one another. Several debates have erupted about AI machines' tremendous data consumption and their art in recent years. Is it possible for artificial intelligence to digest vast databases that contain copyrighted works and then use machine learning to "create" original works without infringing on the rights of third parties? Are the results created by AI protected under intellectual property laws? Machine learning and fair usage are two important concepts to understand. In their endless search for, digestion of, and aggregation of content, AI search engines inadvertently consume copyrighted items such as music videos, songs, novels, and news stories as they crawl around the world wide web. The legality of this digesting, which is usually conducted without the copyright holder's authorization, depends on whether it falls inside an authorized exception to or beyond the scope of copyright law.

The "fair use" exception to copyright law in the United States is the most invoked. As defined by Section 107 of the Copyright Act, "fair use" is determined by considering the following four factors:

- The purpose and character of the use.

- The nature of the copyrighted work.

- The amount and substantiality of the portion used in relation to the whole.

- The effect of the use on the potential market for, or value of, the copyrighted work.

It is expressly permitted by Section 107 to make fair use of a copyrighted work for teaching, scholarship, or research purposes. Fair use is determined by many factors: whether the use is "transformative," as determined by the courts. A fiercely discussed topic that will have ramifications for the future of intellectual property law is whether machine learning of copyrighted information qualifies "fair use."

The future of Artificial intelligence in the Metaverse depends on the interpretation of copyright laws.

A good scenario is Thomson Reuters and West Publishing Corp. vs. Ross Intelligence, Inc. The law firm sued the IT company, alleging that it used machine learning to construct a legal research platform for Ross using the Westlaw database.

Will this be allowed?  Will fair use protect machine learning?

A court recently determined that Google Books' scanning of more than 20 million books, many of which were subject to copyright, constituted a "nonexpressive" and transformative fair use of the texts. The reasoning behind that decision was that it enabled users to find information about copyrighted books rather than the expressions contained within the books themselves.

Protection may be available if the use of copyrighted content is "nonexpressive" fair use, as opposed to "expressive."

Mechanical digestion of copyrighted materials may be permissible if the artificial intelligence (AI) utilized in machine learning is not "too sophisticated." Of course, artificial intelligence has progressed well beyond Google Books. AI can now learn how authors communicate their ideas and then generate their original creative output. This expressive machine learning may, in turn, harm the market for works written by humans.

This expressive machine learning may, in turn, harm the market for works written by humans. Because AI can produce outputs like human expression and personalization, the use of copyrighted works for machine learning may result in copyright infringement, especially if permission has not been secured from the owners of those works before the use of those works.

Metaverse content is being used to train artificial intelligence. This "intellectual property everywhere" scenario is likely to impact how we access and re-use the data created within the Metaverse in the future. As examples of technology whose ability to operate may be hampered in an "intellectual property everywhere" scenario, artificial intelligence (AI) and machine learning (ML) are excellent examples of technology whose ability to operate – given their reliance on ingesting vast amounts of data – may be hindered in an "intellectual property everywhere" scenario.

Data and information used to train a machine learning model may be subject to restrictions in the future. Not all information is "protected" or "owned" for example, protection is unlikely to extend to historical meteorological data, pollution levels, the structure of clouds, or the sound of birdsongs, among other things. Every bird song in the Metaverse is likely to be the work of a computer that a person created, and as a result, it may be able to be protected (for instance, the code used to write the song may be protected, or a human writes the song itself). This could lead to the emergence of new and exciting legal conflicts.

For example, in a world where "intellectual property is everywhere," using nearly any type of information in a machine learning system would almost certainly be considered restricted conduct for which authorization would be necessary.

For example, just "reading" material should not be regarded as a restricted act when it comes to copyright. Still, acts of copying or reproducing – which are likely to occur in the real-world functioning of a machine learning system – almost certainly are, unless a relevant copyright exception is proved to apply, such as the doctrine of fair use in the United States, notable machine learning exceptions in jurisdictions such as Japan, or the more limited (and highly competitive) concept of fair dealing in the United Kingdom Another certainty of the Metaverse is raised by the final point made.

Applicability of fragmented and diversified national intellectual property systems to "international" machine learning and output distribution will be at least as difficult as it has already proven to be in the context of traditional content distribution over the

Internet. This pattern of territorial arbitrage that has marked the evolution of the Internet will undoubtedly reappear in the Metaverse; it is almost likely.

Is AI-created output infringing? Even if the creation of the AI machine learning model in and of itself is not infringing, if the output generated by an AI system that has been trained on a particular type of data is substantially similar, it may be an unauthorized "derivative work" that infringes copyright in the preexisting works. For example, companies like Jukedeck, which was purchased by ByteDance and taken off the market, have used machine learning on recorded music to create algorithms that, in turn, create new music. Because of the potential for companies like Jukedeck to generate automated music that would hurt the market for music composed by humans (such as production music typically used in film or television), these creative outputs will almost certainly receive heightened scrutiny.

Do intellectual property rights protect AI-generated content? In the Metaverse, artificial intelligence (AI) inventions will almost certainly make up a significant portion of the environment – sometimes literally, as in the instance of the Azure-driven location models and maps generated by Microsoft Flight Simulator.

The ownership and rights issues in the outputs of artificial intelligence systems present their own set of issues. Copyright in creative work (and, as a result, its "ownership" and protection) are preconditions for the existence of copyright in creative work (and, as a result, for its protection and "ownership," according to international law. These principles fall apart when the link between a human author and the creative work is broken — most notoriously in the "monkey selfie" case, where an image shot by a monkey was deemed not protected by copyright.

Artificial intelligence-generated outputs (depending on the circumstances, can be distinguished from works made by AI aid) call into question norms that solely consider human authorship of copyright works. Even the United Kingdom's one-of-a-kind provision governing "computer-generated works," under which the person "by whom the arrangements necessary for the creation of the work are undertaken" is deemed the author, confirms the importance of identifying a human rather than a computer as the author of a "creation".

Additionally, traditional reasons for copyright protection, such as rewarding the creation of works or preserving the natural rights of authors, are rendered ineffective when the creator is a computer that requires no incentive and does not have a distinct personality. In short, the legal system in the United

Kingdom does not appear to be welcoming or accommodating of robotgenerated inventions, which (at least for the time being) look destined to fall into the category of free and free-flowing information.

Do you think an AI-generated metaverse has the potential to reshape our world by creating a wonderful environment for the public domain and "commons" to thrive? The question is whether or not an AI-generated metaverse can compete with human-generated worlds in a massive conflict of intellectual property fights. It's possible that the android's doodle of an electric sheep was created by someone else and is not protected by copyright, but the android's programmer may still wish to license it to you.

In the United States, the fundamental goal of copyright legislation is to encourage the creation of new works of art by providing writers with a financial incentive to protect their creations under the law. This economic incentive is provided to authors for the benefit of the public since enabling authors to be compensated economically for their works would produce more innovative content on the Internet.

Will artificial intelligence firms be able to benefit from the economic protections afforded by copyright if they continue to invest in the technologies required for the machine-based production of creative works?

According to Section 102 of the Copyright Act, a work must be "an original work of authorship fixed in any tangible medium of expression now known or later discovered..." to be copyrightable. The need for human authorship is not explicitly stated in either the Copyright Act or the United States Constitution. Still, the courts and the Copyright Office have worked on this assumption. Copyright Office practices require human authorship to register works created entirely by mechanical methods. The Compendium of Copyright Office Practices includes a requirement for human authorship to register works. This case was brought against a wildlife book publisher and dismissed by the Ninth Circuit three years ago because an author who was not human did not have the standing to sue under the Copyright Act. The selfies were taken by a crested macaque monkey and published in the book by a wildlife photographer. This means that once developed, AI-generated works will become part of the public domain and will be available for free distribution.

As things stand, this has significant ramifications for the creation of artificial intelligence-generated works because the firms and investors who fund the machines that make them are currently not protected by copyright laws in the United States. There has been a great deal of debate about whether copyright laws in the United States will evolve to provide this level of protection.

It has been argued that other non-natural persons have been granted legal rights, which supports the extension of copyright protection to nonhuman authors. For many years, corporations in the United States have enjoyed the same rights to contract as individuals and the ability to enforce contracts to the same extent as individuals, in addition to the need to pay taxes. The concept of machine-based work-for-hire doctrine has been advanced by commentators, who argue that the end-user of an artificial intelligence program that generates creative content should be considered the owner of that content.

According to these commentators, the AI program is viewed as the equivalent of a contractor hired by an employer to produce content that the employer owns. However, some have argued that the end user's creative inputs justify the end user's status as a creator of AI-produced content. In contrast, others argue that the AI program should be viewed as a tool for the end-user. 22 Artificial intelligences as a copyright enforcement tool Machine learning, in addition to providing human authors with the power to create new works of art, also offers them the ability to enforce their rights and monetize their works of art better.

Many companies, like Audible Magic and Google, have created artificial intelligence software that detects material and assists in the detection of suspected copyright violations. It is expected that these technologies would provide significant economic benefits to human authors. Should artificial intelligence copyright be based on originality? Some countries, such as the United Kingdom, have taken steps to protect computer-generated works based on the components of creativity embedded within the work to stimulate investment in artificial intelligence (AI) technologies. Certainly, as artificial intelligence advances and generates more "creative" works, the discussion over the ability to copyright these works and who has ownership rights will continue to rage.

Other topics that are receiving a lot of attention in machine learning and artificial intelligence are the ethical compliance of AI systems, as seen by the increasing number of publications and debates in this area. The moral repercussions and hazards of artificial intelligence (AI) are currently believed to be very application-specific. As an example, the potential for in-built biases of an artificial intelligence system to have severe effects on human subjects is thought to be far more apparent in the context of criminal justice applications than in the context of an artificial intelligence-generated piece of artwork. This is at the heart of the European Commission's latest draft Artificial Intelligence Regulation, which identifies "high risk" AI applications that must be subjected to regulatory criteria. Suppose we are to ensure that a Metaverse is safe for everybody. In that case, every AI-generated three-dimensional game environment will likely be free of biases, bullying, and other artificial expressions of violence, which are all too often in our real world environment in the future. If that day comes, all artificial intelligence operators will likely be required to consider their internal processes and governance in light of the high level of safety and security required to enter the Metaverse's construction site. When it comes to ensuring that humans feel comfortable, safe, and at ease in the Metaverse, certain factors should be considered.

Considerations such as the potential for bias in systems and outputs, the quality and nature of training data, the resilience and accuracy of systems, and human oversight and intervention are all essential considerations to bear in mind.

The European Union's Attitude to Artificial Intelligence And The Metaverse

There is no formal EU legal framework for regulating artificial intelligence and the Metaverse. Artificial intelligence development, implementation, and usage are governed by various horizontal laws and principles, including data protection and privacy, consumer protection, product safety, and legal responsibility. The European Commission, on April 21, 2021, announced their long-awaited proposal for a law on artificial intelligence, with the goal of making Europe the global center for trustworthy artificial intelligence (Proposal for a Regulation laying down harmonized norms on artificial intelligence (Artificial Intelligence Act)). The proposal represents the culmination of several years of preparatory work by the European

Commission, including publishing a "White Paper on Artificial Intelligence" in 2012. According to the Commission's vision, the basic rights of individuals and enterprises should be protected and strengthened while artificial intelligence (AI) innovation is encouraged throughout the EU.

<u>Who Is It That the Proposition Is Intended For?</u>

AI providers and users in the EU and providers and users in a third country where the system's output is utilized in the EU would be subject to the new proposed legislation, regardless of whether those providers are situated in the EU or a third nation. What exactly is contained within this proposal? The Commission takes a risk-based but overall cautious approach when it comes to artificial intelligence. While it recognizes the potential of artificial intelligence and the numerous benefits it offers, it is also acutely aware of the dangers these new technologies pose to European values as well as fundamental rights and principles. They adhere to a risk-based approach that may be broken down into four main categories:

Unacceptable risk: Artificial intelligence systems that are deemed to pose an obvious threat to people's safety, livelihood, or rights are generally prevented from being developed. The possibility of psychological or physical injury arises, especially when systems or programs manipulate human behavior to impact the user's free will, resulting in an intolerable danger. For example, toys that use voice assistance to urge youngsters to engage in potentially risky activities would fall under this category of products.

High risk: Artificial intelligence systems that have been recognized as high risk are permitted, but they are subject to additional regulations and conformity tests. Among these systems are artificial intelligence (AI) technologies, which are used in a variety of fields that require higher levels of protection, including education, critical infrastructure, employment management, product security components, law enforcement in cases of interference with people's fundamental rights, and asylum and border control management.

Here are only a few examples of unique responsibilities:

Before being placed on the market, the systems must undergo a thorough risk assessment and mitigation process.

High-quality data sets, complete documentation on all information essential on the system, and its intended purpose must also be provided so that authorities can assess compliance with the requirements. The systems must match the user's needs in terms of transparency and information, and humans must oversee them reduce the chance of failure. This category includes all remote biometric identification systems, subject to the same stringent regulations as the rest of the industry. It is generally unlawful for law enforcement officers to use them in real-time in publicly accessible areas for law enforcement purposes.

Only a small number of rigorous exceptions are permitted, and a legal authority must approve these

Artificial intelligence systems with modest hazards usually are approved, but they must also comply with stringent disclosure requirements.

Users of artificial intelligence systems, such as chatbots, should be made aware that they are talking with a machine to make an informed decision about whether to continue or cease interacting with the system.

Minimal risk

The great majority of artificial intelligence systems, such as video games or spam filters, fall into this category and are legally permitted to operate since they pose minimal or no harm to the rights or safety of users.

<u>What Comes Next?</u>

The European Commission's 108-page proposal attempts to govern a new technology before being widely used. As the world's most aggressive watchdog of the technology industry, the European Union may serve as a model for comparable measures in other parts of the world. There are significant ramifications for major technological businesses that have invested substantial sums in artificial intelligence development and many other organizations that use the software to produce medication or assess creditworthiness. Versions of the technology have been utilized by governments in criminal justice and the distribution of public services such as income support. With such a broad definition of artificial intelligence systems, the rule is sure to have a considerable impact across all industry sectors, particularly in those industries that wish to be successful in the Metaverse. After that, the proposal will be forwarded to the European Parliament and the Member States for consideration under the standard legislative procedure. Given the contentious nature of artificial intelligence (AI) and the enormous number of players and interests involved, it appears unlikely that this will be a simple or straightforward procedure. There will almost certainly be numerous modifications, as well as, hopefully, some more clarifications. It is intended that, once the law is adopted and passed, the rule will be directly applicable in all of the EU's member states.

## How to Join the Metaverse?

Now that we went over the key concepts of the metaverse, let's go ahead and discuss how to become a part of the metaverse. For average users, it will be as simple as putting on their headsets and using an internet connection. However, you may want to seek a career related to the metaverse, or you may want to start a business and get a bigger slice of the pie before the market gets saturated. Even today, both are attainable goals, and considering the metaverse will influence the future, the time to plan is now.

You have two options if you want to work in the metaverse or start your own business: You can either join the ranks of infrastructure creation, or you can build on it. One is not better than the other, and the choice purely depends on what you find more exciting.

The obvious benefit of working in the metaverse infrastructure is its stability. As of now, the metaverse is being built by tech giants with a crystal clear vision of the foreseeable future. If you choose to work for them, you will not only be working on exciting new technology, but you will also receive competitive pay and benefits. Furthermore, you will be able to gain invaluable experience and know-how during your tenure that will come in handy should you want to start your own business later on.

However, the metaverse is clearly more lucrative when you start a business. Until the metaverse business becomes saturated, you have a great opportunity to become one of the first entrepreneurs to enter it. We will explore the infrastructure and market aspects of the metaverse for career and business opportunities. Let us begin by talking about some ways that you can be involved in the metaverse's creation.

<u>Creating the Metaverse</u>

You can work for the metaverse infrastructure in a number of ways. The creation of the metaverse will consist of hardware, software, and content.

<u>Hardware</u>

Despite the fact that hardware is one of the building blocks of the metaverse, it is one of the least discussed. Part of the metaverse is about experiencing 3D environments in the most realistic way possible. Due to current technology, we need external hardware to assist us in doing this. Virtual reality glasses are often associated with Facebook's Oculus, a story of inspiring entrepreneurship in and of itself.

Oculus glasses were first envisioned by Palmer Luckey when he was just 15 years old. This is a great example of how your passion can turn into a billiondollar business. Luckey was interested in the earliest versions of virtual reality glasses, a curiosity triggered by his fondness for console gaming. Early virtual reality glasses were introduced in the 1980s and 1990s. In those days, they were either too expensive or did not work at all, so they all failed as business models. Luckey started collecting these failed products as a hobby. Little did he know that his hobby would develop into a deep understanding of virtual reality glasses.

He created a Kickstarter campaign to build virtual reality glasses. The idea behind his campaign was to gather money for hardware parts and to create about a hundred virtual reality glasses. The campaign had a modest expectation of $250,000. However, the Kickstarter campaign raised much more than that. Within 24 hours, Luckey raised $680,000. In just three days, that number exceeded a million and caught the eye of game development giants like John Carmack and Gabe Newell. In 2014, they were acquired by Facebook for a whopping $2 billion. It seems that Zuckerberg's Meta was already beginning to boil then.

Luckey's story teaches us a valuable lesson about entrepreneurship in uncharted territory. First of all, timing plays a big role. Virtual reality glasses weren't Luckey's invention. They were invented decades before. What changed was that Luckey had technology behind him to identify what wasn't working and create what would work. Secondly, it is the idea that matters the most, not necessarily the product itself. Luckey's affinity for virtual reality led him to success, not his prototype that he put on Kickstarter.

In conclusion, creating a hardware business around the metaverse comes down to the first economics lecture every student has: supply and demand. You need to anticipate the demand and when it will begin. Once the market is ready, supply innovative solutions that are affordable to the vast population. Remember that hardware is the bare minimum a user will need to have to enter the metaverse. Therefore, it will always be essential in the supply chain, and you will have many opportunities to participate.

<u>Software</u>

Software is the bread and butter of the modern-day world. The online world wouldn't offer us all the opportunities it does without it. It goes without saying that software development will be important in the metaverse for both online and offline applications. You can work in the software industry or start your own software development company.

The good news about working in the software is that metaverse positions are already available in the present. Companies like Facebook, Google, Apple, and Snap are hiring software developers to work on their share of the metaverse. If you are not a fan of corporate jobs, you might consider working for new startups that emerge in the metaverse including Roblox, OpenSea, Decentraland, Niantic, The Sandbox, and Solana. There will always be a great demand for software developers of all levels in the industry.

When it comes to steering your career toward the metaverse, some programming languages are better than others. Augmented reality, virtual reality, blockchain, and cryptocurrency all require different programming languages. Your choice will be influenced by which part of the metaverse you are interested in and which language you are comfortable using.

There is a good reason why C# and C++ have been around for decades. Their object-oriented nature makes them popular choices for game development. Millions of people around the world use 3D game engines like Unity and Unreal to create environments. Another language to consider is JavaScript, which gained popularity in Web 2.0 and will do so again in Web 3.0. If you're interested in developing Web applications, JavaScript is a great option. Lastly, we can't forget about Python, the newest kid on the block. Python's open-source code base and scripting abilities make it ideal for virtual reality, which is why companies like Oculus choose it. Even if you don't plan to work for anyone else, you will still need these languages to develop your own software.

It is best to team up with like-minded people if you intend to create your own software based on the metaverse concepts since you will need to work fast and get ahead of the competition. Don't get too ambitious about competing with the big names because they will never be completely transparent about their R&D. After all, they are competing with big names themselves. Your hard work can go to waste if they drop a product you didn't know existed overnight. Instead, focus on supply and demand. What are some specialized areas that big players won't touch? Build your business centered around those niche areas.

## 3D

All aspects of building a metaverse we discuss are vital, but 3D is the real foundation. The reason is quite simple: We perceive in three dimensions. If we lived in Carl Sagan's *Flatland* that would be a different story. However, the human brain processes the world in three dimensions, which means virtual reality must be constructed accordingly. Even if another form of reality existed, we couldn't perceive it, so the users couldn't benefit much from it.

3D's popularity predates the metaverse. However, the low-polygon Lara Crofts is a thing of the past. As computer processing power improves, 3D technology continues to evolve. Ray tracing technology from NVIDIA is a fantastic example of this. It is very close to creating environments that are similar to real life, if not there already.

Metaverse companies stand to gain the most from the 3D aspect of the technology. However, because 3D is safe and predictable, there will be fierce competition. Don't wait for content mills to take over the market before you reap the benefits of 3D. Get your studio or freelance service set up as soon as possible, and take advantage of social media to build a network and increase your popularity.

Picking a niche is the key to success as a content creator. When designing 3D environments, you will have many different choices. Authentic designs are well suited to architecture, corporate simulations, and hardcore game development, while cartoon-like designs are well suited to early metaverses and casual game development. There are pros and cons to each side, so choose whichever style fits your interest and talent. After that, you can go ahead and choose a niche. Your niche could range from hyper casual game development to military training. Keep doing what you enjoy, as it will help you stay motivated.

You can also take on the software aspect of 3D if you want to push the envelope. A 3D artist needs software such as Maya in order to create and render their work. In the last decade, there were also 3D modeling programs such as Blender that were able to be used by anyone to create 3D models without being an artist. Both have become industry standards. There is an exceptional chance that a program that directly imports metaverse APIs will prove valuable because they are the ones more likely to become industry standards.

<u>Community Management</u>

Compared to software or hardware development, community management may seem insignificant, but that's short-sighted. Effective community managers will become one of the most important assets of any metaverse. We need only look at the forum culture of Web 2.0 to understand this.

When early forums hit the web, they were all the rage. For the first time, people from all over the world were able to share their thoughts. But most importantly, it was the first time they could do it *immediately*. Certainly, this paved the way to freedom of information. There were, however, some hard lessons along the way. It was unfortunate that we had to learn these lessons after real-life crimes were committed using internet anonymity.

Moderators and administrators were first used at that point. They were chosen from among users who spent significant amounts of time on the forum and who wanted to contribute their free time to it. This brought the concept of 'vetting' to the internet. Essentially, a moderator's job was to respond immediately to user input. Additionally, they could monitor a user's personal messages. As time went on, different online communities developed different policies. Although some opted for total freedom, while most of them strictly prohibited hate speech.

However, if an internet dispute crosses over into real life, it's always a tricky situation. A lot of debate has occurred regarding whether a crime committed online can be prosecuted in court. Governments were not prepared for this, which resulted in internet regulations that continue to be murky to this day. Just ask Facebook CEO Mark Zuckerberg, who had to explain how social media works in front of the House Financial Services Committee.

You can enter this line of the metaverse in a few different ways. You can consider the legal side of the metaverse if you're interested in pursuing a career in law. A corporate route is an option, as big tech names are willing to pay good money for lawyers who understand where they are coming from. Other options include working for NGOs and lobbyists.

Again, if the law isn't your dream career, consider software. With over a billion accounts on their hands, companies like Facebook don't have the option of hiring moderators, although they do that as well. The real goal is to develop artificial intelligence to take over this job for them. Therefore, community management is one area that won't let you down if you are interested in developing artificial intelligence. The options are not limited to big companies either. You can create a great enterprise if you combine artificial intelligence with consulting options for small and medium businesses.

<u>Finance</u>

Another area that will build the metaverse is finance. Better yet, almost anyone can contribute to this aspect of the metaverse. The only requirement is a passion for the metaverse, an open mind, and financial literacy, which can be learned on your own. Learning these skills will lead to wonderful opportunities.

Metaverse economies are prone to volatility due to their decentralized nature. This fact presents two business opportunities. First of all, you can work on a private blockchain to create a less volatile cryptocurrency. This is no easy task, but if you can create the right team and lead them with the right vision, it is perfectly achievable. Keep in mind that R&D requires significant time and money investments, and it could take a long time. On the other hand, a method that gives some stability to the volatility of the virtual economy would be a game-changer.

The second and quicker way would be to become a financial advisor. In order to become a financial advisor, you should consider a college education, although it isn't mandatory unless you plan on working in official means. Providing valuable predictions in a volatile economy is invaluable for both personal investments and portfolio management. Furthermore, since there is still some controversy around cryptocurrencies, some people have gone so far as to call them akin to gambling. Metaverse economies are still a novelty, enabling users to make incredible profits. But as the number of metaverses grows, they will need services to make their economy more stable. Additionally, governments will wish to regulate them to ensure tax compliance.

Therefore, you do not have to go down the traditional finance world road. Instead, you can take a software-focused approach. With a good understanding of blockchains, you can provide a wide range of services to meet the new demands a new economy will bring. In addition to creating unique blockchains, you can also develop innovative smart contracts. You can then customize templates for user agreements and privacy policies, all of which are essential to Web 3.0.

Lastly, you can simply create economies. The process of creating and maintaining a cryptocurrency is a team effort, but making altcoins isn't so hard. This business requires a lot of visibility, though. It is estimated that there are a little over 5,000 altcoins as of the start of 2022. Crypto circles refer to these coins as 'shitcoins' because they don't function properly and have no value. That doesn't have to be the case. Remember Dogecoin? It created a lot of millionaires when Elon Musk got interested in it. Getting Elon Musk onboard for your PR campaign isn't always feasible, but we can learn from this experience. It can work just fine if your altcoin serves a purpose and establishes a name for itself in the right circles.

## Joining the Metaverse

Creating a metaverse might not be your cup of tea, but you can build on what's already been created. Listed below are some ideas that will change certain industries and lead to new employment and business opportunities.

## Event Planning

Virtual reality will revolutionize the way events are organized. You can offer virtual events as one of the early studios to offer this service. The events can be anything from concerts to seminars. For your virtual event planning business to succeed, you will need to do three things: organize, promote, and ensure the software is running smoothly.

You can work with event planning companies or start your own company by teaming up with other creatives. It depends on the type of event you're planning. You can probably use a virtual reality builder for private parties, seminars, and concerts. You will need some coding skills, however, if you want to take your events to the next level.

Think of Star Trek's famous Holodeck. On the starship Enterprise, everyone's favorite part is the Holodeck. No surprise there. It's a blank 3D environment and you can run whatever program you want. You can become Sherlock Holmes, travel in time to discuss mathematics with Einstein, and visit different planets. Basically, you can use your imagination to the fullest. If you're looking for this kind of customized event planning, you will need some serious software to back you up. It is precisely for this reason that giants like Google seek engineers to work on their augmented reality projects. Augmented reality will be the future of event planning in Web 3.0.

<u>Consulting</u>

Being a consultant is a perfect fit if you have a deep understanding of the metaverse. The consulting industry in the digital era has evolved in an interesting way. As we discussed before, when Web 1.0 hit, the big names were unaware of just how important it would become. Just ask Yahoo, who had to spend $5.7 billion to acquire Marc Cuban's broadcasting website. They could certainly have done better if they had a competent consultant in their corner.

Start preparing now if you are interested in becoming a consultant for the metaverse. Make sure you stay on top of the latest developments and learn how to analyze data if you haven't already. Network as much as you can and work on your cold pitches. Assume the role of a metaverse consultant through blogging, social media, or as a guest author.

Right now, many business owners are feeling nervous about Web 3.0. They do not want to repeat the Web 2.0 mistakes and you can make a huge difference for businesses. There is no need to wait for the widespread adoption of virtual worlds and blockchains. The use of smart contracts, cryptocurrencies, NFTs, and virtual land is already available and can be incorporated into any business.

Start an NFT agency for artists who are looking to protect their digital copyrights. Provide affordable smart contract programming services. Contact investment networks and offer to be the link between them and metaverse start-ups. Hold seminars on investing in cryptocurrency. Finding something you enjoy, understand, and believe in about the metaverse is the key. The business idea will follow.

Virtual Real Estate

Since the dawn of time, real estate has been a lucrative career and investment opportunity. The logic behind real estate investment is simple. The earth is not going anywhere. A valuable piece of land will always hold its value and provide opportunities to build on it. A similar approach is true for the metaverse virtual lands. What makes these lands even more exciting is that they are limitless. As long as users build virtual worlds, there will be virtual lands to buy, sell, and build on.

You can choose to specialize in virtual land and real estate in a number of ways. One of the more obvious ways is to become a virtual land agent. You can act as an intermediary between landowners and those who are looking to invest in the virtual world. At the beginning of the metaverse, users will likely feel compelled and anxious at the same time. After all, virtual land is different from what they already know. If you possess communication skills and financial literacy, you can become an invaluable asset. Virtual land is very valuable.

A different approach would be to become a contractor. A metaverse engineer would have different capabilities. The Golden Gate Bridge is an outstanding example of modern engineering, but in a virtual reality where the laws of physics can be altered to mimic whatever you want. The possibilities are truly endless. Just look at Minecraft! The business model is already in place. Through SimLab's virtual reality creation software Composer, users can already create environments tailored to their needs. Their customers include impressive names like NASA, Tesla, Nike, Sony, and Volvo.

Lastly, we can't forget about land flipping. Flipping land successfully requires getting used to the virtual world first. Once you know the land, and where people are likely to spend their time, you can invest in virtual land. This will require some capital, but if you are able to add value to your land, it will pay off nicely. Establishing a business on your land will increase its value and make it a popular location to display advertisements. The key is to be creative. When the land value has reached its maximum potential, you can sell it and invest in larger land to begin the process all over again. Another alternative is to rent the property or hire a contractor to do the work for you.

<u>Virtual Business</u>

Using the data available, we can assess the small business potential of the metaverse. In its prime, Second Life had a blossoming economy of small businesses. People have taken advantage of this by creating side hustles, and some have even been able to turn them into full-time jobs.

In most virtual worlds, people enter the digital environment with an avatar. As our avatars, they can do everything that we can in reality, and more. In addition to eating, sleeping, and seeking entertainment, they go on vacation, work, socialize, and form romantic relationships. Luckily, you will be right there to meet those needs.

Your metaverse business doesn't have to be intricate. Even something as simple as opening a coffee shop on a busy street can be very successful. One of the biggest benefits of operating a business in the metaverse is that you will earn in-game currency. The money can be kept as a cryptocurrency or cashed out into fiat money. You can generate additional income by hosting events like stand-up comedy and live music jams. Coffee shops also make great meeting places. You can offer other businesses and users a job board at your coffee shop or rent out space for advertising.

If you want, you can always go the Second World route and customize highend items. There is no reason why you can't be the Gucci of the metaverse. The interesting thing about virtual worlds is that users build emotional ties with their avatars. They perceive them as a better reflection of themselves. Popmundo, a popular virtual roleplaying community that allowed users to become rockstars, was a great example of this. In spite of not making any actual music, you could manage your bands' artistic and financial affairs. People were willing to pay for VIP services just to have better avatars. Users spending irresponsible money on/as their avatar is a relatively rare occurrence and one you shouldn't exploit. For the average user, buying some items for your avatar here and there is quite common. Most people will want items that not every other user has. You can play this angle and make a decent amount of money.

The coffee shop and the custom item boutique are just two examples of small businesses that could thrive in a virtual world. You are only limited by your own imagination. Nevertheless, you may be compelled by the metaverse businesses without wanting to hold an entire operation. The good news is that you don't have to start a business, you can just invest in one. Towards that end, we will explore the business side of the metaverse.

# Invest In The Metaverse

Like any other investment opportunity, Investing in the Metaverse requires careful calm consideration and logic.

Investors are encouraged to think carefully and deeply before deciding on which investment strategy to employ.

<u>What Are Investment Strategies?</u>

Investment plans are techniques that assist investors in determining where and how to invest their money based on their projected return, risk appetite, corpus amount, long-term versus short-term holdings, retirement age, the industry of choice, and other considerations. Investors can tailor their plans to meet their specific aims and aspirations when it comes to investing.

Investment strategies can be divided into five types. Let's take it one at a time and go over the many types of investment methods.

<u>Passive and Active Investment Strategies</u>

The passive technique is purchasing and storing coins rather than exchanging them regularly to avoid greater transaction costs. Because they believe they will not outperform the market due to its volatility, they prefer passive tactics, which are less hazardous. On the other hand, active tactics entail frequent purchases and sales of products. Investors feel they can outperform the market and earn higher returns than ordinary investors believe.

<u>Growth Investing (Short-Term and Long-Term Investments)</u>

Investors choose the holding term based on the amount of value they want to add to their portfolio. To increase the corpus value of a token, investors must believe that the token will grow in the upcoming years and that the intrinsic value will increase. This is referred to as growth investing in some circles. On the other hand, short-term investment is made when investors feel that a token will offer good value within a year or two of the investment. The preferences of the investors themselves also determine the holding time. For example, how quickly they require money to purchase a home, send their children to school, or fund their retirement plans, among other things.

<u>Value Investing</u>

The value investing technique includes investing in a token based on intrinsic value rather than the market value since markets undervalue such companies.

Investors in such companies hope that, when the market undergoes a correction, the value of such undervalued companies will be corrected, causing their prices to skyrocket, providing them with substantial profits when they sell their shares. Warren Buffet, the world-famous investor, employs this method.

Income Investing

Coins in this sort of approach are chosen for their ability to provide cash flow rather than for their ability to grow the overall worth of your portfolio. Cash income from this form of investing can come in two types: fixed income (through yield farming) or dividend income (staking)

This technique is preferred by investors searching for a consistent stream of income from their investments.

Investing in Dividend Growth Companies

Tokens with a track record of routinely paying interests are more stable and less volatile than other companies, and they strive to improve their dividend payout each year. In this strategy, the investors reinvest the earnings and reap the benefits of compounding over the long run.

Investing Guidelines for Beginners

The following are a few investing tips for beginners that you should consider before making a financial investment.

Set Financial Objectives

Establish financial objectives for how much money you will require in the upcoming period. This will enable you to determine if you need to invest in long-term or short-term investments, as well as the amount of return you may expect to receive.

This will enable you to determine if you need to invest in long-term or short term investments, as well as the amount of return you may expect to receive.

Investigation And Trend Analysis

Before investing, take the time to thoroughly research how the market operates and how various financial instruments function.

Additionally, analyze and monitor the price and return trends of the coins you intend to invest on.

Portfolio Optimization

Choose the most appropriate portfolio from the portfolios that best fit your objectives. An ideal portfolio generates the most significant return while posing the least amount of risk.

Risk Tolerance

Determine the level of risk you are willing to accept to achieve the desired return. This is dependent on your short- and long-term objectives as well. You would seek a more significant rate of return in a shorter period, while you would seek a higher risk in reverse.

Risk diversification is essential. Invest in different projects to diversify your risk and increase your returns. In addition, be sure that both tokens are not associated with one another.

Advantages Of Investment Strategies

Investment Strategies Have several Advantages. Some of the advantages of investment techniques include the following:

- The use of investment methods, which invest in various investments and industries based on time and expected returns, allows for risk diversification in the portfolio.

- When constructing a portfolio, investors can choose from one strategy or a combination of methods to meet their specific tastes and requirements.

- Investing wisely allows investors to make the most of their money and maximize their returns.

- Investment techniques can help you save money by lowering your transaction costs and paying less tax.

Limitations To Investment Strategies

Examples of investing methods' drawbacks include the ones listed below:

- Investors of average means have a difficult time outperforming the market. Even though cryptocurrency is a great project to invest in with remarkable and fantastic rewards, many new beginners still struggle to see tangible results in the sector due to a lack of patience and greed.

• Even though a great deal of study, analysis, and historical data are considered before investing, most decisions are predictive.

• It is possible that the results and returns will not be as expected, which will cause the investors to be further behind in accomplishing their objectives.

• It is critical to have a well-thought-out investment strategy. It will assist you in weeding out bad portfolios and boost your chances of becoming successful.

• Consider a few fundamental questions, such as how much money you want to put into it. What kind of return do I require? What is the extent of my risk tolerance? What is the length of my investing horizon? Why was it necessary for me to invest?

• The more specific your objectives are, the more confident you will be in your ability to make sound investing decisions. Always be on the lookout for potential investment opportunities and never make a large sum of money at once.

- Building a portfolio is like building a house from the ground up, brick by brick and dollar by dollar. It is best to do it right rather than do it fast.

# What Will the Metaverse Change?

The metaverse is not only bound to change the world as we know it but the way we view it. With the implementation of 3D worlds, we will have infinite possibilities for work, travel, entertainment, and more. Let's have a look at some of the ways we will use the metaverse in the future.

<u>Travel</u>

The metaverse will play an important role in travel in the future. Putting on our glasses will allow us to see anywhere on earth without having to travel. The world of 3D modeling and rendering has changed drastically over the past decade. In the past, rendering and shading realistic 3D models was extremely resource-intensive, and the results were heavy graphics. Nowadays, not only do we have better 3D production methods, but our graphic cards and internet connection also process them much more quickly and efficiently.

Leading companies like Unity and NVIDIA are already developing cutting edge 3D graphic technologies that look extremely realistic. These graphics are currently used mainly in video games, but they are gradually making their way to the movie industry. Eventually, we will have video services that will allow us to travel anywhere in the world. Better yet, we won't have to deal with crowded landmarks and may choose any weather we like.

There will be more than just real-time travel in the metaverse. One of the most exciting features of the metaverse will be time travel. Though technically we will only travel to the past we know, it is a start. Imagine traveling to the "Seven Wonders of the Ancient World" or interacting with prehistoric hunter-gatherers. The possibilities are endless.

Metaverse travel will be perfect for those who love travel but can't due to certain limitations. Professionals who work full-time and have limited time off, parents who cannot travel with young children, elderly people who have physical limitations, and people with disabilities are examples of lives the metaverse travel will change.

<u>Entertainment</u>

The entertainment industry is about to undergo one of the greatest changes with the upcoming metaverse. We can expect the entertainment industry to become much more interactive and accessible.

For example, the metaverse can change the way we listen to music. Artists can create music videos in the metaverse and sell tickets to their studio sessions. In addition, the size of the venue won't matter for ticket sales. The metaverse can take live concerts to the next level. We won't be restricted to a specific time or place to watch our favorite artists, and we certainly won't have to wait for our favorite bands to go on tour.

This is also true for the movie industry. Our favorite movies and television series can easily be metaverses on their own. You could ride a dragon beside Daenerys Targaryen in the Game of Thrones metaverse or enter the Matrix for the ultimate *metaverseception*. We might see a scenario like this in the latter stages of the metaverse, but interactive movie experiences are likely to be available in the initial stages. Companies like Disney and Lucas Arts already own the intellectual property rights to their universes, so they are in a good position to create a metaverse based on their franchises.

Adult entertainment is another example that is expected to benefit from the metaverse. Some experts claim that the adult industry is expected to reach $122 billion in 2026. The introduction of new internet technologies to adult entertainment is nothing new. There are many websites offering video clips and webcam interactions to their customers. The adult entertainment industry has proven to be crisis-proof, and the metaverse is sure to add its own twist to it.

Another industry that is enthusiastic about the metaverse is the gambling industry. In 2021, online gambling generated $230 billion and remained one of the most lucrative markets for online enterprises. Decentral Games, for example, offers virtual gambling using NFTs and their DG coin. We can anticipate this trend becoming more popular as the metaverse expands.

<u>Military</u>

The military is one of the few low-profile investors in the metaverse. Keeping up with the latest technology is a necessity for the armed forces to stay in top shape. In addition, armed forces around the world rely on simulations to train their personnel. Because the metaverse will create realistic simulations, it is only natural for the military industry to take advantage of it.

Optimus System was one of the first companies to jump on board. Their company develops and supplies military training simulators. DEIMOS, their new metaverse technology, is preparing to enter the global market. Their system creates military training environments like precision shooting, tactical behavior training, and observation training. Optimus System CEO NamHyuk Kim said: "We plan to expand the development of scientific products to implement more effective, real war-like training systems based on the technologies of the fourth industrial revolution. Our company will lead the global Metaverse market with new ideas and differentiated technologies."

Military war games and training cost organizations like NATO billions of dollars every year. With the help of metaverse technologies, not only would they be able to reduce their budget, but they could also create highly realistic training scenarios without endangering personnel.

E-commerce

Web 2.0 has made e-commerce a part of our everyday lives. Numerous business owners transitioned to digital, and countless others developed lucrative side businesses via e-commerce stores. Online deliveries have become the norm and kept the world going during the Covid-19 pandemic.

We can expect our online shopping habits to evolve with the arrival of the metaverse. The stores can create their own metaverses or come together to create virtual shopping malls. We can walk into these stores and check out the real size, color, and fit before we make the purchase.

On the other side of the metaverse, shopping will take place in the virtual reality economies themselves. Virtual land, tokens, and other goods unique to each metaverse will be available to us with cryptocurrencies. Currency for a metaverse can be Bitcoin, altcoins, or a completely original token.

Whatever the case may be, the metaverse will have a business opportunity in e-commerce. By deciding on the type of products you want to sell early on, you will have the opportunity to be among the first to enter the market. So, if you have an original idea or product, you should consider patenting it.

<u>Workplace</u>

Several tech giants like Microsoft have been working on creating a metaverse for the workplace. The initial plan is to create virtual conference rooms where colleagues could meet using virtual reality. During the pandemic, online meetings have already become commonplace in the workplace using apps like Zoom and Google Hangouts. Employees have felt the effects of what's called "Zoom fatigue," and companies are looking for better ways to engage employees online.

Through the metaverse, an online conference room will become much more realistic. The presentations will be more compelling, communication will feel more genuine, and the audience will be more engaged.

As metaverse workplaces prove to be useful, they could greatly increase the number of international teams. Furthermore, companies can hold their international meetings online and reduce their business travel expenses. Although the metaverse cannot completely replace human interaction, it can certainly speed it up. You can create a business that offers an international working hour scheduling service or create a translation plugin for international meetings. That is two excellent business models for the metaverse right there.

<u>Gaming</u>

Gaming will be one of the industries to cross the frontier into the metaverse. Virtual reality glasses caught the attention of the gaming industry when they were introduced. These days, popular game engines like Unity 3D offer developers to export their games for virtual reality. Moreover, 3D art and environments have been used in the industry for decades. We can expect game developers to be among the first to adapt to the upcoming metaverse.

They will be able to adapt quickly beyond the technical aspects of game development.

Games with large followings, such as MMORPGs and MOBAs, have utilized their own currencies for in-game purchases for a long time. A few developers are now accepting cryptocurrency payments too.

The gaming industry has all these advantages over other industries, making it one of the poster children for Web 3.0. You can invest in the metaverse early on by investing in game studios that are shifting towards it. If you are a high risk investor, look for angel investment opportunities in small startups. To be on the safe side, look for established game studios that are showing signs of making the shift. Collect stocks early and follow them regularly to ensure they are progressing.

Dating and Relationships

Online dating has changed the way we meet people many years ago. Nowadays, meeting someone is as simple as logging onto a website or downloading an app on your phone. We can only anticipate the metaverse to shake things up even more.

Remember that artificial intelligence and machine learning are crucial parts of Web 3.0. Dating applications like Tinder and OkCupid are wildly popular because they match us with people we're already interested in. This not only saves us time but increases the chances of a first date going well.

We can expect to see this on a larger scale once the metaverse starts influencing the dating world. Artificial intelligence will make smart guesses about our preferences. Whenever we express a liking or disliking for a specific trait, our choices will create a compound pool of characteristics we will be interested in.

We will be able to meet these people right away in the metaverse, which is even more exciting. Using this technology, we will be able to interact with people deeper without having to share personal information like phone numbers and addresses. This should make online dating a safer experience in the future.

Another group that will benefit from metaverse dating is long-distance couples. Some couples start off long-distance, and some evolve into long distance relationships due to work like army officers. The metaverse era will give these people a chance to skip the Skype call and spend meaningful time with their loved ones.

Do you have a Christmas tradition of watching a certain holiday movie? Even when you are thousands of miles away from your loved ones, you can join the metaverse and watch the movie together. It doesn't end there. You can teach your children how to play chess, take your spouse on a two-hour date to Paris, and catch up with your friends on a virtual pick-up game. In the metaverse, you can do all of this and much more.

Media

Previously, we discussed the impact of information decentralization. One of the biggest industries to be affected by information decentralization was, undoubtedly, the mainstream media. Newspapers and news channels initially viewed the internet as a way to spread their accessibility. However, they took one of the biggest hits in the process.

Information democracy brought by the internet allows users to both generate and consume the information they want. Among the biggest reflections of this statement are the social media apps we use every day. Furthermore, the internet gives alternative media a fair chance to compete with mass media. As a result, the press no longer has a monopoly. A similar situation applies to big TV networks that have lost market share and influence to streaming services like Netflix.

It is hard to predict what Web 3.0 will bring to the table as far as the media is concerned. Web 3.0 is about us being able to see our input reflected back to us. Media outlets on the entertainment side might find it easier to adapt to Web 3.0. However, it remains unclear how the 24-hour news cycle will interact with Web 3.0. Governments will no doubt take action against the complete decentralization of news, as they do today. However, it can be speculated that self-journalism and social media will become more prominent. We will likely have more access to personal news stories that artificial intelligence thinks we will be interested in. In addition, there could be ways to set trigger alerts or mental health precautions based on what we consume. To date, Time has taken the boldest step into the metaverse from a media outlet. They are launching a weekly newsletter solely dedicated to the metaverse.

<u>Education</u>

The Covid-19 pandemic has proven that face-to-face education is not the only way to learn. While online education has its own challenges and setbacks, the metaverse can offer solutions. Using the metaverse, teachers can interact with children in virtual reality, which is a far cry from a Zoom call. Even more impressive, a teacher can instruct any student in any part of the world by means of machine learning techniques and translation technologies.

The metaverse has the potential to revolutionize education. Imagine yourself sitting in your Seattle home and taking a leisurely stroll in front of the Eiffel Tower with your favorite French teacher. Taking a school trip to Germany to learn about World War II without getting on a plane. Learn painting from Leonardo Da Vinci himself. Observing the human body from inside. These are a few examples of what virtual reality and artificial intelligence can do for the education system.

We can expect schools throughout the world to have metaverse campuses in the future. A few examples are already underway. A virtual campus will be created, for instance, at the Kenya-KAIST campus, which is expected to open by September 2023 in the Konza Technopolis. The University of Nicosia is preparing to open the first permanent university gallery for NFTs. They will also start offering a six-week course "Introduction to NFTs and the Metaverse," which starts in February 2022 as a part of their UNIC Open Metaverse Initiative. Over time, these examples will multiply and become more complex, resulting in student exchange programs being a daily occurrence.

Another group that will benefit from the educational implementation of the metaverse is students with disabilities. As a means of bridging the education gap between able-bodied and disabled students, augmented reality will be invaluable. It will be easier for teachers to design personalized activities for disabled students, and long-term hospitalization will not hinder academic success as much.

There is no doubt the metaverse will impact all industries one way or the other. What matters is how we respond to it. By embracing the metaverse early on and exploring its potential, we can take advantage of this wonderful technology and not let it pass us by as it changes the world.

# Crypto Metaverse Projects

This chapter will discuss the top 5 cryptocurrency projects relating to the metaverse and how to invest in them.

1. SANDBOX

What Is the Sandbox token and How Does It Work? The Sandbox (SAND) is an Ethereum-based ERC-20 token that serves as the native asset of the Sandbox virtual economy. It is traded on the Ethereum exchange.

SAND tokens will be 3 billion, with around 900 million tokens already in circulation.

For a project that prides itself on being decentralized, it is surprising to find that most of the entire supply is allocated to the corporation, its personnel, advisors, and investors. In addition, the token performs two essential services on the platform at the time of this writing. In-game things can be purchased in the marketplace with this currency, staked to generate interest.

The Sandbox team's editing program is the backbone of the game. The software allows users to construct 3D objects such as creatures, costumes, buildings, automobiles, and pretty much anything else they can think of in their minds. A non-fungible token (NFT) is created for each item, which may then be sold on The Sandbox's marketplace or secondary markets such as OpenSea.

The ability to develop whole 3D games that can be played within the virtual world without knowing how to code is also available. You can monetize your games and earn SAND every time someone plays them if you're determined to make money from this enterprise.

The Sandbox game is played on a vast map divided into segments, which the developers refer to as LAND.

A single NFT is worth thousands of dollars, and each piece is sold as a standalone. Many gamers have turned into virtual real-estate tycoons, enhancing their plots with stuff purchased from the marketplace and reselling them.

Lands can be combined to form larger and more valuable estates and districts due to their geographic proximity. It is possible to make money with your land in ways other than simply flipping it, so explore your options. You can host events and games, charging a price for admission and hoping to attract many paying customers.

According to the inventors, SAND will eventually serve as a governance token and a cryptocurrency.

According to the project's whitepaper, a decentralized autonomous organization (DAO) will be integrated into The Sandbox by 2023, at the earliest. The SAND holders would vote on issues that affect the future of the game and ecosystem once this process is completed.

It's difficult to conceive an utterly decentralized Sandbox because the bulk of tokens and voting rights are likely to remain in the hands of the company, its crew, and its backers. A significant portion of the platform's token supply may be made available to the public in the future. However, as of now, the token's decentralization is still in its infancy.

The Price History of The Sandbox

The announcement by Facebook to rebrand itself as Meta was by far the most significant event in the history of The Sandbox's price.

The token had only achieved an all-time high of $1 in September, just before the announcement. SAND had been trading at around $0.05 per share for several months until late January 2021, when it began to join the rest of the market in the incredible 2020-2021 bull-run that started in late January. It reached its first significant high in March, at approximately $0.85, just a few months before Ethereum reached its all-time high in May.

Even though its rise to $0.85 and then $1 was spectacular, it was outdone during the first week of November, when it soared to $3 in a matter of days.

Following Facebook's announcement, the value of tokens such as SAND surged. On the surface, this attitude appears to be completely logical.

As more people become familiar with the technology, the existing platforms may see a significant increase in use. In contrast, Facebook has now announced that it will be developing what will undoubtedly be the most formidable competitor to The Sandbox. A tech behemoth has entered the space, most likely intending to destroy the existing ventures with a figurative steamroller.

Decentraland is expected to be Meta's most significant competitor until Meta's Metaverse is released.

On the surface, the two initiatives appear to be highly similar.

These two games are metaverse games centered around a cryptocurrency and have an NFT-based economy in common. However, there are significant distinctions between the two of them. Using their groundbreaking 3D editing software, The Sandbox allows its customers to create practically anything they can imagine.

Decentraland is a little more straightforward for the typical person, but that may be more appealing to them.

Decentraland also has a significantly higher number of active users at the time of writing and appears to be receiving a little more brand recognition.

For example, Coca-Cola Co. (NYSE: KO) has decided to begin selling branded NFTs in the game as early as this year. Although the Sandbox boasts many noteworthy partners, such as Atari and Snoop Dogg, it appears to be falling behind its competitor in this area.

How To Buy Sandbox

Because the Sandbox token is a relatively popular cryptocurrency, it may be found on several notable cryptocurrency exchanges. FTX and Gemini are two of the best trading platforms for the token, and they both support it. It is also sold on other exchanges like Binance and KuCoin.

The success of SAND will most likely be determined by how well players receive it in the future. Even if the Metaverse becomes a hugely popular concept, The Sandbox will require people to participate in the game and contribute to its ecology to succeed.

The Sandbox has the potential to be a terrific investment. For confident investors, it has already been shown to be such.

If you had purchased it in January, your investment would have increased by about 5,000 percent. It is, nevertheless, an exceedingly risky investment, as are most cryptocurrencies.

If the game cannot attract users and investors, the price of SAND will almost certainly fall over time. Whether The Sandbox will be a major player in metaverse games within a year is tough to predict. Still, it is likely a better bet than some of its lesser competitors.

<u>In What Way Does Purchasing a Piece Of Land In A Sandbox Benefit You?</u>

A decentralized community-driven gaming, visual art, and game design environment built on the Ethereum blockchain, Sandbox allows makers and designers to create and commercialize their new functionalities (NFTs), art experiences (including gaming observations), and gaming observations (including NFTs).

One of the most important goals of Land areas is to provide a platform for game developers and designers to expose experiences on them that can be played and monetized by gamers.

Various other services, such as leasing out land and making land claims, will be available.

There are two types of land available for purchase: standard and premium.

How To Buy Land on Sandbox

Sandbox sells land via public auctions of real estate. The announcement is made in the official communities in front of the public.

Before purchasing a plot of land from the Sandbox, you must first register with the site.

The map may be found on Sandbox's official website, where those interested in purchasing land during public property sales should go.

To purchase a piece of land, select it from the list of available parcels.

It will be indicated in yellow if there is any accessible Premium land. In contrast, it will be displayed in grey if there is any available standard land.

The "Buy" button, highlighted in blue, should be used if you wish to acquire the land.

Until the sale is finalized, canceled, or fails to proceed (for example, because of a lack of natural gas), the land would be held in reserve (after two hours).

After then, the land would turn purple, signifying that it had been reserved.

Your bank account should indeed be displayed, prompting you to complete the payment and explicitly explain the quantity of gas (charged in ETH) that you are now spending in your transaction.

It will be completed as soon as your bank account receives confirmation of the payment. The amount of gas you choose and any blockchain congestion significantly impact the time it takes to execute the transaction.

When you are successful, the land will become red to indicate that you have now acquired ownership of it.

<u>How Does Buying Land on Sandbox Make You Rich?</u>

Lands on the Sandbox, a type of digital real estate that allows you to generate a very clean and consistent source of revenue, will give you multiple options to make a very clean and constant stream of income.

Let's look at how the land can make you a very wealthy individual.

Hospitality Industry

Users can host living experiences like games, art museums, stores, scenery, engaging education, and other activities on Sandbox. The primary role of property is to allow users to host live experiences.

Sandbox's own game development program, known as the Game Maker, may be used to design and build these experiences, which can then be made available on any of the creator's territories. Players may be required to pay an entrance fee in cryptocurrency to access the experience offered on the land.

Staking

Landowners will be able to stake cryptocurrencies on their lands in exchange for passive incentives in the future, thanks to a feature planned for Sandbox.

One of these perks is GEMs, an ERC-20 token that is extremely valuable and sought after by asset design professionals.

As a bonus to the regular staking incentives, these GEMs can be sold on the open market in exchange for cash. Your Land area ownership functions as a multiplier when you deliver SAND-ETH cash flow to a UniSwap liquidity provider, increasing the amount of SAND cryptocurrency you receive from cash flow mining.

It will also be possible for renting landowners to lease their properties to third parties, such as game designers and film production firms, who may have missed out on a property during the original sales.

Upon the completion of the sale of all available land, the quantity of available land for rent will surge as more individuals become aware of The Sandbox and opt to submit an experience there.

## Contests and Giveaways

Organizing contests and giveaways on land might bring a significant number of paying buyers to your property to participate in the competition or giveaway. Other people may conduct tournaments or give away prizes on your Lands to promote their businesses and increase your exposure.

## Advertisements

Are you an affiliate marketer? Do you own a business of your own? Are you a published author? Are you a creative person? For that matter, anyone interested in selling a product or service. Then why not widen your reach by utilizing some of your advertising space on your property to market yourself to players and visitors who might otherwise be unaware of your product or service.

## Asset Non-Financial Transactions

Whenever you decide to publish an experience on your property, you will develop admittance requirements and a price for visitors to participate in it.

It is possible to impose an entrance requirement that players first hold a specific asset, such as NFT, as one of the prerequisites. Suppose a player wishes to participate in your land-based swashbuckling pirate game but hopes to purchase a weapon from your worldwide NFT sword collection, which you also released on the global market.

Land For Sale in The U.S.

The sale of land inside Sandbox is, of course, an additional opportunity to generate money, mainly if the land is in a high-traffic and highly sought-after zone of the Metaverse.

In the long run, however, if you can maintain your composure and hold onto your Land regions for a longer period, you will most likely earn more money through a combination of the various strategies discussed in this article.

What Is the Cost Of Land On Sandbox In Dollars?

The cheapest land available for purchase on Sandbox is more than 10000 USD.

The average price of land has increased significantly in the last three months. The average land price increased from 40 USD to 960 USD in less than a year.

<u>Is There Risk Involved?</u>

There is, without a doubt, one. As a result, proceed with caution. Land prices may decline in the future. It is still in its early stages and has not yet gained widespread acceptance. However, given the current trends, it is doubtful that we would see a significant decline in the price of land. However, now would be an excellent moment to purchase it if there is. Sandbox is a company in which I have a lot of confidence. Looking forward, it will be intriguing to see where life takes us.

The Metaverse is the future, and any investment in land within Sandbox or other Metaverses could turn out to be a terrific venture soon. The reward to risk ratio is high. According to estimates, the price of sandbox land can climb by 5-10 times in less than a year.

Nothing, however, can be guaranteed. This is not financial advice. Do your research.

2. DECENTRALAND (MANA)

Who is Decentraland, and what does it do?

MANA is the ERC20 fungible cryptocurrency token developed by Decentraland. MANA is the currency used in Decentraland's in-meta economy.

The land is bought and sold with MANA in mind.

Decentraland, a virtual world framework, is powered by the Ethereum blockchain. Consumers can produce information and software, experience it, and monetize it. The community owns the property in Decentraland for all time, allowing them to have complete control over the area's development. Users can claim ownership of digital land using a blockchain-based parcel record. Property owners can regulate what information is released on their parcel of land, defined by a set of cartesian coordinate systems (see image below) (x,y). The type of information can range from static 3D scenes to interactive systems such as video games and simulations.

For many investors, the act of purchasing land in Decentraland represents a significant step forward. It is a fantastic technique to increase the amount of money you have. In the same way that real estate is unique, each property portion is represented by a non-fungible token (NFT, ERC 721), which means it cannot be crafted or recreated, much like real estate. In addition, Decentraland offers the option of obtaining a mortgage on the land.

Anyone, at any time, can buy, sell, or lease land peer-to-peer on the official Decentraland Global market or through Opensea. You formally and indisputably own that plot of land when you hold that land token, which is possible because all operations are processed on the Ethereum platform as honest proof-of-purchase. If you decide to invest and build in Decentraland, you should know the following information.

Renting an offline property is expensive, and Decentraland offers a more cost-effective way to own a piece of real estate. The following options are available to those who wish to invest in this platform:

Purchase a piece of real estate

Landscape design

Shop

Start your own business.

Play video games set in the real world.

Socialize and converse with others.

<u>What Can You Buy at The Decentraland Marketplace? What Can You Do In Decentraland?</u>

In the Marketplace, you'll find everything you need to trade and manage your Decentraland tokens.

Land parcels, estates and clothing, and distinctive brands are all available for purchase globally. You can set your MANA price as well as a deadline for submitting proposals.

On Decentraland, you can purchase real estate tracts and estates, as well as wearables and one-of-a-kind names that are for sale.

<u>How To Purchase Land in Decentraland?</u>

Anybody can buy, sell, and lease land on the Decentraland Marketplace or Opensea at any given time. In addition, Decentraland offers the possibility of securing a mortgage on the land itself. In Decentraland, to be precise.

You can obtain a bird's-eye view of every color-coded property/plot, estate, street, region, and plaza in the Decentraland Marketplace using the Atlas View. You may move about the map by clicking and dragging it using the mouse. You can also zoom in and out and hover your mouse pointer over a parcel to display its x, y coordinates, and owner. Any parcels currently available for buy on the global market will be highlighted in this website section. Tap on a parcel to learn more about it, including its status, coordinates, and the public address of its owner (if it has an owner). You could also make a buy or an offer on the displayed parcel from this screen.

<u>What Is an Estate On Decentraland?</u>

An estate, like land, is a digital asset that cannot be exchanged. An estate is a collection of two or more pieces of land located close to one another. These parcels must be adjacent to one another and cannot be separated by a road, plaza, or any other parcel of real estate. You might manage your greater huge estates more effectively by connecting parcels to develop Estates. For example, estates are handy for creating larger sequences that span numerous pieces of land.

<u>What Exactly Is a Parcel, Anyway?</u>

Like real property, every land parcel in Decentraland is a non-fungible token (NFT, ERC 721), which means that it is unique and cannot be solidified or recreated, exactly like it is in a cryptocurrency.

The cheapest piece of land in Decentraland is 3487 MANA.

<u>Where To Buy Items on Decentraland?</u>

The Explore tab will take you to the Marketplace View, where you can see all of the currency for sale. Select the Category option if you just want to look at a specific type of item.

Sort them according to various criteria, such as the most recent, the least priced, and so on.

To keep an eye on products that aren't for sale, turn off the sale feature.

Sorting the products by title will help you find what you're looking for.

How To Buy MANA Tokens

This is a straightforward procedure. Once you've logged into your existing account, click on the "Exchange" or "Markets" link to access the trading platform. Then browse for currency pairs of interest to you, such as ETH/MANA or BTC/MANA, among others. A "BUY" button will appear below, where you can enter the amount of money you wish to spend or even the amount of MANA you want to purchase to proceed. You can purchase MANA tokens by filling out the form on this page.

The following items can be purchased in Decentraland: land, estates, wearables, and one-of-a-kind titles, among others.

Land Prices in Decentraland

The total land area is 90,601 hectares, with 43689 private property parcels, 33886 district land, 9438 roadways, and 3588 plazas. Private land parcels account for 33886 hectares.

Each plot of land has a square area of 16m x 16m, whereas earlier, it was 10m x 10m

The most expensive piece of land ever sold was for 2,000,000 MANA.

The average price of land has increased from less than 500 USD to more than 3000 USD in the last five years alone.

<u>Is It Worthwhile to Invest in Decentraland Real Estate?</u>

The future of Decentraland is based on the number of people who show up and subsequently use the platform. Many people are drawn to this cryptocurrency as a pure digital interest and hope that it will become a legitimate digital currency, like Bitcoin. One of the most major advantages of Decentraland is that it allows users complete ownership access to their virtual assets and properties. This feature distinguishes it from other virtual reality systems on the market.

The money generated and the people who use their land are retained by the proprietors of the digital world's real estate properties. This differs from other systems because it involves a cut of profits. Because the plan is decentralized, there is no centralized authority to oversee or control it in the traditional sense. As a result, purchasing virtual land in the Decentraland Metaverse is a fantastic long-term investment.

Purchasing and selling land on Decentraland entails a certain amount of financial risk.

There is, in fact, a monetary danger. So please exercise caution. In the long run, the value of land may decline. It is still in its early stages and has not gained widespread adoption. Nonetheless, given the current trends, it is doubtful that we will see a significant decline in land prices in the near future. Now would be a wonderful moment to invest if there is a market for it. Decentraland is undoubtedly one of the top coins to look out for as the metaverse develops.

## 3. STAR ATLAS

In your opinion, when was the last time a AAA game made its roadmap public, released a game iteratively, and engaged in blockchain-native sales? Right, never. What is Star Atlas?

With its open-world, space exploration, and grand strategy elements set in an alternate universe, Star Atlas is an MMORPG that emphasizes player ownership and play-and-earn features in its galactic setting. Players pilot ships and participate in trade, commerce, and combat with other players over limited resources. The company wants to construct a AAA game using the Solana blockchain. This tier 1 blockchain system can handle 50,000+ transactions per second. This will be critical in dealing with the large quantities of transactions in-game, where players will mine and explore, pay taxes, and trade assets — all of which will be powered by Solana and settled on Serum, a decentralized exchange — and will be handled by Solana.

In its biggest ambition, the game strives to be:

• A space-fantasy RPG featuring a real-money economy and NFT assets.

• A grand strategy game involving politics, trading routes, and economically productive territory.

• A 24/7 virtual economy where users may come together in realtime to trade, make contracts, and participate in the battle.

It is possible to explore a completely realistic 3D world with film-quality graphics, driven by Unreal Engine's Nanite, in virtual reality.

Star Atlas has been profiting on the tremendously hot fundraising market for blockchain games. In addition, they announced Animoca Brands as one of its stakeholders, hosted town halls, and published a blockbuster teaser for the highly anticipated game. This corresponds to the first round of their nonfungible token (NFT) pre-sale as well as the launch of their Galactic Asset Offering (GAO) (GAO).

Furthermore, a significant part of the attractiveness of Star Atlas is the opportunity for players to feel like they have ownership in a video game while also being able to monetize their skills, enthusiasm, and effort. Star Atlas is enticing to many players who dream of making a living inside an immersive video game universe. A player can make money by stealing from traders and then selling their stolen goods for $ATLAS (Star Atlas' token) on the marketplace and exchanging that $ATLAS for fiat money.

Key Features

Territory And Exploration

Star Atlas is a game about space and spatial exploration. Initially, players will start at a corner of the map. They will survey the visible stars for celestial and earthly valuables. These basic assets can be refined and exchanged, and sold, just like any other commodity. Those who travel towards the center of the map are rewarded, but with reward comes risk: players may lose their hardearned riches if they don't act quickly enough. Traveling and transporting things in Star Atlas takes time, which opens new markets for logistics, freight, and even infrastructure, such as bridges, as a result.

A Virtual Economy and Society That Is Strong and Resilient

Among the features planned for Star Atlas is a complex virtual economy in which players can make economic decisions about cargo shipping, travel, fuel management, and defense powering. Player earnings can be obtained ingame through various roles, according to their whitepaper. Here's a sample of what you can expect: "CEO, Bounty Hunter, Repair, Freight, Rescue, Refiners, Miners, Managers'. "Managers are accountable for ensuring that resources are utilized efficiently to create value and utility," according to the authors of an economics article on the metaverse. Power Plant Manager and Salvage Operator are two examples of management-type jobs."

Star Atlas Cryptocurrency Tokens

$ATLAS and $POLIS are the two primary currencies offered by Star Atlas. $ATLAS is an inflatable currency intended for selling in-game assets. At the same time, $POLIS is a low-velocity store of value with a fixed supply (we've seen this model before in Axie Infinity's $SLP and $AXS). While $ATLAS is acquired (and spent) within the game through fighting and exploration, $POLIS empowers players to own and manage space cities. It also reflects a financial investment in the game and governance powers over in-game topics like land tax rates.

Star Atlas aspires to be a physical embodiment of the blockchain, not just in function but also in appearance. In its whitepaper, Star Atlas defines the fundamental mechanic of the game: mining. You stake out celestial and earthly properties claims, and then you start mining the resources. This is accomplished using an NFT ship. A decentralized exchange (Serum's onchain order book) is used for trading any assets you produce. This allows Star Atlas to support its development by potentially taking a share of secondary sales while also protecting the uniqueness of player assets by assuring that no assets can ever be replicated or destroyed.

Star Atlas' Future

The latest NFT ship sale by Star Atlas may have netted the company more than $20,000,000, but there is still a lot of work to be done. The blockchain will force Star Atlas to maintain grey markets open. In contrast, Star Citizen secured many funding rounds over several years and deliberately clamped down on them. This means that any player dissatisfied with the game can quit and take their money with them. They intend to contribute the USD collected from their ship sales to an ATLAS: USDC automated market maker, which is now under construction. As a result, this money is available to gamers who wish to exchange their in-game currency for other digital goods.

Additionally, Star Atlas has received all-star backing from various sources, including Animoca Brands, Serum, and Moonwhale Ventures. They will provide their DeFi and NFT gaming expertise to help take Star Atlas to the highest level possible.

Moreover, they have a significant AAA gaming partner in Sperasoft, who has collaborated on notable titles such as Star Wars: The Old Republic, Star Wars: Battlefront II, and most recently, Halo Infinite, among others. Being able to rely on a partner with AAA development experience will be critical for Star Atlas' long road ahead. Their recent increase may help them devote additional resources to developing the Star Atlas universe.

In the end, Star Atlas intends to release its game in parts, with the first of them beginning on Monday with the first round of their Galactic Asset Offering (GAO), in which they auctioned ships on their marketplace, which Serum powers.

Star Atlas Roadmap

The CEO of Star Atlas, Michael Wagner, commented that as from November 2021, players and members of the STAR ATLAS community could begin earning from next month by engaging in the second phase: a web-minigame that allows users to use some of their assets and that an immersive 3D environment will be available to explore by the end of the year.

The gamers will begin familiarizing themselves with the game mechanisms and remain involved with the game when released. Typically, AAA games take too long to receive input from their players and the gaming community. Eight million pre-orders for Cyberpunk 2077 were based only on anticipation and trailers before players had a chance to see any of the gameplay elements.

Star Atlas's approach surrounding release flips the conventional secretive development process on its head: offering public information about gameplay mechanisms, marketing its pre-sales, and facilitating a 58,200-person large Discord group. This has its perks. Players can begin immersing themselves in the universe, taking up roles in the Discord (Mercenary, Bounty Hunter, CEO…), and forging alliances and guilds. They can even seek support onboarding into crypto from other prospective players and keep each other interested in the game.

Clicking Play Now on their landing page sends you to their marketplace. The founders have stated that their economy and speculating and trading will be a significant game component. However, it may be a concerning indicator if gamers are more interested in flipping ships than flying them. Moreover, conventional gamers may get disinterested if they are confronted with the prospect of making payments and trading even before they enter the game.

Star Atlas will be the first AAA game to show how NFTs and digital asset ownership can fund game development and operations. By being the dominant liquidity source of $ATLAS and $POLIS, they should support the game's development. This will be a significant step forward in legitimizing play-and-earn as a viable business model for game creators and publishers.

Star Atlas is an enormously intriguing project, but with great potential comes significant risk. If played correctly, Star Atlas can educate game designers on how to employ actual digital scarcity to enhance gamers' experience by offering a play-and-earn metaverse where they can win rewards for their efforts. To see this idea through, their 55-person production team, their partners Hydra Studios and Sperasoft, and their 58,200-member Discord community must work together.

## 4. ILLUVIUM

AAA blockchain games seem to be the focus for metaverse crypto coins. Illuvium is one such token.

Illuvium is a cross between an open-world RPG and an auto battler, with an economy built on collectible NFTs and resource mining as its primary sources of income.

Will Illuvium be the first AAA blockchain game? That is what Kieran and Aaron Warwick, the company's co-founders, seek to do.

A claim like this has been made numerous times in the brief history of nontraditional gaming (NFT). On the other hand, Illuvium has acquired a substantial pace since 2020.

In just six months, the game reached the milestone of 100,000 Discord subscribers. In addition, between July 2021 and October

2021, the ILV token's value increased from \$30 to \$700, thanks to the token's introduction on major exchanges such as CoinSpot.

The gameplay experience promised by Illuvium and the game's tokenomics is present in even greater detail than usual.

Is Illuvium possible to be one of the finest NFT games of 2021?

Illuvium is slated to enter open beta in the first quarter of 2022. However, that is already a delay from the third quarter of 2021. As far as we can tell from the limited video available as of September 2021, the Q1 2022 release date appears unrealistic.

Not every region presents the same level of challenge or even accessibility. There is a free-to-play foundation Tier 0 realm that can be explored by anyone who wishes to do so. It helps you become more familiar with the game's mechanics and the concept of tracking down and collecting Illuvial. You can mine for free Shards, which can capture the most fundamental Illuvials in the game.

However, if you want to advance to the Tier 1 and higher regions (it appears that it goes all the way up to Tier 5), you will have to spend some money on it. You'll make your payment in Ethereum (ETH).

<u>What Media Formats Does Illuvium Support?</u>

Although you can lock in PC and maybe Mac, there have been no announcements regarding formats. Illuvium: Zero is a mobile spin-off game currently in development. The current aim is to mine resources for the main game while on the go.

<u>What Is the Premise of Illuvium?</u>

Illuvium starts with a very familiar adventure-themed premise.

In Illuvium, you role-play a member of the intergalactic space fleet in a drastic position. Your ship has crash-landed on a disaster-ravaged planet. The ocean has swallowed most of the land, and what little land remains is being pummeled by natural calamities. Enormous obelisks, erected by some past residents, have blocked the entrance to some locations totally, and giant obelisks have completely blocked access to others.

Your objective is to figure out what caused this catastrophe to occur while also unlocking the obelisks along the way. For this, you will need to mine the soil for Shards, which can be used to capture Illuvials and subdue them so that they can be employed as soldiers in your private army.

Illuvial are God-like creatures that inhabit this unnamed planet, fueled by radiation and performing miracles. You can think of them as being very similar to the Pokémon franchise. Or, at the very least, Pokémon has been given a mature kicking in the shins, removing some of the corny Nintendo lusters in the process.

At the beginning of the game, you will have the option of customizing your character's appearance. As a bonus, you will have the option of selecting a drone to accompany you on your quest as a sidekick. PSD stands for Polymorphic Subordinate Drone, and it is a type of drone.

Illuvium bills itself as an open-world role-playing game, putting it on par with titles such as The Elder Scrolls or Cyberpunk 2077 in terms of scope. If it was AAA, that is. Early footage reveals a 3D world with huge environments loaded with a reasonable amount of detail and a reasonable amount of detail. It's created with Unreal Engine 4, a middleware solution that is exceptionally robust for this type of game. Furthermore, the color scheme is reminiscent of the most popular game powered by that engine, Fortnite.

Although the founders have promised a variety of locations, however, they have only released a few glimpses of what they might look like so far mainly in the form of concept art – so far.

Some film of a barren rocky island, surrounded by beaches and ocean, has been posted on the internet. However, it appears bland and linear for something meant to be an open world. In addition, a day-night cycle has been proposed.

Traveling around the overworld is accomplished on foot or by passing through the Obelisks dispersed throughout the globe. Towns can also be found near these Obelisks, which will allow you to construct new equipment and serve as a haven against Illuvial.

As you go over the terrain, you will come across Illuvials, land-based creatures. These aren't free-roaming creatures but rather ones who come and go from the earth. Which is a fancy way of stating they just appear out of nowhere during random bouts. This gameplay mechanic can be found in vintage Pokémon and Final Fantasy games. You won't be able to track them down like you would with Monster Hunter.

You can engage in combat with Illuvial. If you are victorious, you will have the opportunity to capture them in a Shard.

Suppose you're attempting to capture an Illuvial. In that case, your chances of success are determined by two factors, namely: the abilities of your Shard and the power of the Illuvial you're trying to capture. Captured Illuvials become a part of your collection, which you can use in future battles. The better and stronger your group, the further you can proceed through the game's various levels.

<u>What Are Illuvials, And How Do They Work?</u>

The Illuvial is the Pokémon of this world, and they have a lot of power. Alternatively, you could call them the Axis. There are over 100 to collect, which is a tad lacking in quantity. Pokémon Sword and Shield, for example, had 400 points. The Illuvial are classified into one of five affinities (water, earth, fire, nature, and air) and five classes (water, earth, fire, nature, and air) (Fighter, Guardian, Rogue, Psion, and Empath). They also have three life phases to progress through, from cubs to deities, during which they can level up.

However, as you go through the game and encounter rarer and more powerful Illuvials, you will find that they can have various affinities and classes. It's also possible to fuse three fully leveled Illuvials, resulting in new variations with rarer powers. The game also rewards players who amass extensive collections of Illuvials like one another, allowing them to "synergize" and increase their abilities.

Adding an extra curveball to the mix is a rare occurrence in photography. The use of a Shard increases the likelihood that it will mutate into a Shiny, Rainbow, or Holo form, each becoming increasingly rare as time passes. These modifications alter the appearance of the Shard and increase its value in the eyes of the NFT's owner.

This capture procedure appears to have some interesting (albeit not unique) depth on paper, which makes it worth mentioning. While those in search of some uncommon (read: valuable) NFTs have something to look forward to from the Fusion concept, Illuvials will also level up during combat, so they will potentially improve as they are utilized in-game, which is something to look forward to from the Fusion concept.

Every time you capture an Illuvial, an NFT is created in your account. It is possible to develop an Illuvial by joining three NFTs together; however, the three existing NFTs are destroyed. However, it is unclear if the outcome of a Fusion is determined by chance or by design.

<u>What Is the Battle System Like In Illuvium?</u>

It is no coincidence that Illuvium's fighting draws inspiration from the auto battler genre, which is a new gameplay experience that only gained traction a few years ago. Auto Chess was the game that started the trend. Still, Dota Underlords, Hearthstone Battlegrounds, and Teamfight Tactics are all crucial inclusions in the list.

An auto battler is a video game where you do not directly control the actual battling in real-time. Instead, it's all about teamwork and planning of time. Use your Illuvials in this scenario, to be precise. What kind of Illuvials have you amassed? What methods did you use to enhance them and provide them with resources? The numbers, rank, class, and type of your formed team are all critical, but how do they interact with one another? Each Illuvial has a fundamental, critical, and final attack that must be considered as well.

Then, of course, these techniques must be evaluated considering your opponent's advantages and disadvantages as well.

Illuvium Vs. Pokemon.

In this sense, the gameplay is highly like that of a card collecting game (CCG). Alternatively, it might be a Pokémon title. On the other hand, with an auto battler, after the pieces (read: Illuvials) are placed on the battlefield, you can step back and observe in a passive capacity to determine if your pre-fight strategy was successful. It is not yet clear how many fighters you will be able to bring into each battle, but screenshots indicate that you will get eight Illuvial.

Lastly, it's important to remember that your player character is always on the battlefield. While the player is a spectator in battle, their avatar actively participates. It can add affinity and class auras to your Illuvial team, which will improve the attributes of your assembled group of Illuvial.

Also available is the option to bond your character with an Illuvial, which will grant even more additional bonuses. This hasn't been fully explained yet, but it is described as semi-permanent for the time being. It suggests that while taking this route may allow you to capture more Illuvials because you have a more powerful team, doing so may deflate the value of that NFT or even cause it to be burned as a sacrifice.

Resources Derived from Mining

Your drone is employed to extract minerals from the planet's surface. It is possible to find ore, uncured Shards, and jewels, all of which are of variable rarity. These can be utilized to make new armor and weapons and improve those you already have on hand. The changes you make here affect the auras your player character emits in battle, affecting the boosts that your Illuvials receive.

You can also harvest organic materials from the trees found all around the earth. These can be given directly to Illuvials to provide limited-time enhancements while in combat. One such example allows you to gather toxic goo, which may be used to boost the attack stats of Illuvial.

What Kinds of Game Modes Are There?

At the game's debut, there will be only one mode available: Adventure Mode. A large portion of the gameplay described above takes place in this mode. We may expect two battle arena modes to be released following the game's introduction: Ranked and Leviathan. The former levels the playing field for skill-based matches, whereas the latter does the opposite. The latter is a freefor-all where you can bring whatever collection you want to share.

It's worth noting that the creator has stated that he intends to allow for ingame betting on the battle arena and arena mode. It will be interesting to see how governments worldwide react in response to this!

<u>What Are Shards?</u>

As you've no doubt guessed, Shards are the Illuvium equivalent of the Pokéball. It is necessary to mine these from the ground in uncured form. How The quality of the Shard you recover is random in terms of strength – or, to put it another way, random in that the stronger the Shard, the more uncommon it is. To capture powerful Illuvials, you'll need powerful Shards. As a result, if you venture out without a few decent Shards up your sleeve, you face the possibility of encountering an Illuvial that you are unable to capture.

<u>Who Is Behind the Development Of Illuvium?</u>

Unfortunately, the developer of Illuvium has chosen to remain anonymous, as has been the case with many other developers in the NFT and blockchain gaming field. Moreover, this is usually a red indicator in my book. Further worries are raised while looking at the two co-founders. Kieran and Aaron Warwick are brothers from Sydney, Australia, who have no previous experience in the game production industry.

Kieran, the first, is a successful entrepreneur. Aaron has never worked in a game development environment despite his many years of experience as a long-time coder enthusiast. The greater crew has a combined total of relatively little noteworthy gaming experience. Nate Wells, a former employee of Irrational Games (BioShock), Crystal Dynamics (Tomb Raider), and Arkane Studios (Dishonored), is the only notable name on the list. He only serves in an advisory/producer capacity.

This does not rule out the possibility of them creating a fantastic game. Still, one should be skeptical of any first-time developer who claims to revolutionize NFT gaming by releasing a AAA title.

The game is being developed on the popular Unreal Engine 4 middleware solution. The tokenomics are all anchored by the Ethereum ERC-20 blockchain, just to be clear. Immutable X oversees dealing with non-financial trading (NFT).

How To Make Money on Illuvium

Because this is non-financial-transaction gaming, the primary means of making money in Illuvium is collecting and selling high-value Illuvial. However, for the player to access the most valuable and rare Illuvials, they must delve deep into the game's world.

To accomplish this, players must mine rirrf3ri Shards from the world's land, unearthing ore, and gemstones that can be used to upgrade and improve gear and harvest organic resources from plants that can provide in-battle buffs, among other things. All of this happens while you're capturing, leveling, and fusing an Illuvial team that's capable of taking on and capturing the rarest (read: most valuable) creatures you can find.

Accordingly, players can trade resources they have gathered, weapons and gear that they have crafted, or lesser Illuvials to other players in markets that have been set up for this purpose.

In-game transactions between players are carried out entirely using the ILV token. IlluviDEX is the marketplace name where all these transactions occur, and Immutable X. operates it. This is a third-party, layer-2 Ethereum transaction engine that allows for the transfer of NFTs without any gas.

Furthermore, it should be noted that there is a limited amount of Illuvials in the game's ecological system. As more of a type is discovered, the more difficult it becomes to locate them.

However, there are plans to include more areas and Illuvial in the future. It will be fascinating to watch how they handle the addition of new holders without depreciating or aggravating the existing holders.

Even while it will not be available at launch, gamers will eventually place wagers on ranking matches in the battle arenas. However, it appears that land purchases are related to the Illuvium: Zero mobile spin-off game, as indicated by the fact that they are listed as "coming soon" on the website.

## How Much Does It Cost to Participate In Illuvium's Events?

While in-game trades between players are conducted using ILV tokens, all transactions between the game and its players are conducted over the Ethereum blockchain. You will never require ILV to participate in the game.

There are two methods in which Illuvium can take Ethereum away from a player. The first is that they charge a 5 percent fee for any transaction between two or more players. (An additional 0.5 percent fee is charged, split between Immutable X and the user.)

In-game items can be obtained through the purchase of in-game items. The following are the five things you can purchase with ILV tokens:

Shard Curing

Shard Curing is a technique for transforming mined Shards into Illuvialcapturing Shards.

Travel

Using an obelisk to travel between different locations.

Crafting

If you want to get better equipment quickly, this is the way to go.

Cosmetics

If glitter and looks are your things, go for it.

Revival

If you don't want to wait for a wounded Illuvial to mend, you may use ETH to speed up the procedure. This tactic harkens back to the dreadful monetization methods used in mobile games.

It's unclear at this point how much it will cost in ILV to cure a Shard, but this is at the core of the game's monetization strategy. Without Shards, you will be unable to capture any Illuvial.

Illuvium's Tokenomics

At total dilution, the maximum number of ILV tokens traded on the market will be 10,000,000. Before the game's debut, 9,000,000 coins will be in circulation, with the final million coins being distributed as in-game incentives and for winning tournament matches. The DAO already has 1,500,000 more tokens in its treasury, which will be used to reward players for completing in-game objectives and participating in tournaments.

There are 2,000,000 ILV tokens delivered during seeding, which will be unlocked in March 2022 and then drip-fed out at a rate of one-twelfth of a percent every month for the next year. It is also planned to drip-feed the 1,500,000 ILV tokens held by the team at that time but a pace of 1/36 every month for the next three years.

Illuvium Tokenomics is a new kind of economics. According to the time of this writing, another 3,000,000 tokens are currently being locked away in yield farming for 12-month vesting stints (June 2017).

Those who purchase ILV have the option of staking them in two locations. On the one hand, the direct ILV pool is expected to earn an annual percentage yield of 85 percent (APY). Alternatively, there is a secondary LV/ETH Sushi Liquidity Pool on Sushi.com – where you must stake both ETH and ILV 1:1 – where you can invest more money. This results in an annual percentage yield of 600 percent on the combined sum.

However, because of the opportunity for token owners to claim their share early by converting ILV to sILV, the ultimate pool of 10,000,000 ILV tokens may never be reached. In-game spending of this synthetic alternate token, which has a 1:1 value to the main token, allows individuals who have staked their ILV to do so before their funds are unlocked. Any ILV that was used in these transactions was destroyed.

Holders of ILV will get a full refund of all earnings generated through the Illuvium game, including interest.

The Illuvium Distribution System

Illuvium is a DAO.

The Illuminati Council is elected every three months, with five community members being elected to the positions from among those who have put themselves forward. The square root of an individual's ILV stake is used to determine their voting power. As a result, one ILV equals one vote, 36 ILV equals six votes, and so on. This is done to avoid over-dominance by whales and seeders.

The council has the authority to "discuss and distill technical modifications" and consider dividing the 1,500,000 ILV currently stored in the treasury. Any changes to the protocol, known as Illuvium Improvement Proposals, must be approved by a supermajority to be implemented.

<u>Where Can You Buy Iluvium?</u>

You can currently purchase Illuvium on the following cryptocurrency exchanges:

CoinSpot

CoinSpot is an Australian cryptocurrency exchange that makes it simple to buy, sell, and trade more than 290 different cryptocurrencies.

Binance

This cryptocurrency exchange was founded in 2014. Binance is the largest cryptocurrency exchange globally in terms of the trading volume. Get started with zero-fee AUD deposits and withdrawals in Australia. Take advantage of minimal trading costs, a diverse range of cryptocurrencies, and local customer service available 24 hours a day.

Cointree

This cryptocurrency exchange operates in the United States. Other exchanges where you can buy Illuvium include:

- KuCoin
- Crypto.com

- Gate.io
- OKEx
- Bithumb Cryptocurrency
- Hotbit Cryptocurrency Exchange

What Is Illuvium: Zero, And How Does It Work?

Illuvium: Zero is a spin-off title to the Illuvium series that will be released on mobile devices in 2022. It's a city-builder, where players can buy a plot of land and then build out a civilization that can mine minerals.

If you are playing Illuvium: Zero for free, those resources are tied to the Illuvium: Zero game and cannot be used elsewhere. However, if you have purchased the game, the resources you mine can be transferred to the main game and used as fuel to aid you in your pursuit of Illuvials in the game's primary mode. Also available is the ability to scan Illuvials who roam your property and use the information gathered to make skins that can be sold to the public as blueprint NFTs.

Illuvium appears to be a promising prospect on paper. When it comes to the collectible Illuvials, there is a clear progression and rarity tree and a clear plan for a developing economy. The combination of 3D exploration and auto battler combat should be particularly effective in Unreal Engine 4.

However, there's very little game development experience in the team and no serious footage of gameplay in action to back up the proposed expertise.

As always, whatever you decide to do, invest wisely as this is not financial advice.

5. $UFO

WHAT IS UFO token? Social gaming coin UFO Gaming is decentralized and may be used on any platform. P2E (Play to Earn) Metaverse, Virtual Land, NFT, Gaming, and IDO Launchpad.

The $UFO token will be needed for all $UFO-related activities. For any interaction with the ecosystem, this is required.

The token may be used in three ways: $UFO, UAP, and Plasma Points.

If you stake $UFO or $UFO-ETH in the Cosmos, you'll get Plasma points, which may be redeemed into UFOep.

Our initial game, 'Super Galactic,' requires Origin UFOep to run.

- UAP is needed to buy, trade, and fuse (breed) NFTs in the game. Playing Super Galactic is the only way to get this item.

To access some of the most anticipated gaming projects, you must stake your UFO tokens or purchase property on a dedicated planet.

There are several chains in our Dark Metaverse. Several chains will be used. UFO's games will cover various genres and niches, launching on some of the most respected chains.

Interoperability across games on the same planet. On June 30th, 2021, UFO was made available for trading. It has an undetermined total supply.

Coins like Bitcoin and Ethereum may be acquired using fiat money on crypto exchanges, but not UFO. We'll show you how to buy UFO by first purchasing Ethereum on any fiat-to-crypto exchange and then transferring your funds to the exchange that trades this currency.

First, you'll need to get your hands on one of the most popular cryptocurrencies, like Ethereum (ETH).

The second step is to buy ETH using a currency other than ETH.

Third, transfer ETH to an altcoin trading platform like Bitfinex.

UFO may be traded on various listed exchanges, so visit each and sign up for an account.

Below are some examples of exchanges that currently possess the UFO token while writing this book.

- Gate.io
- MeXC
- Coinbase
- Binance
- 1-inch
- ShibaSwap
- Uniswap between UFO and WETH (V2)
- UFO/WETH

In addition to the exchanges listed above, there are several well-known cryptocurrency exchanges with large user bases and good daily trading volumes. As a result, you'll be able to sell your coins whenever you choose and at a lesser charge. As a result, if UFO is listed on one of these exchanges, a significant amount of trading volume will be generated by its customers, providing you with excellent trading chances!

## Binance

Binance was founded in China, a prominent cryptocurrency exchange, but later relocated to Malta, a crypto-friendly EU island. The crypto-to-crypto exchange services provided by Binance are well-known. After bursting onto the scene during the 2017 crypto frenzy, Binance has become the world's most popular cryptocurrency exchange. Binance does not accept US investors.

## Gate.io

Gate.io is a cryptocurrency exchange based in the United States founded in 2017. If you are a US investor, you may trade on this exchange since it is based in the United States. Both English and Chinese versions of the conversation are accessible (the latter being very helpful for Chinese investors). Gate.io's wide range of trading pairs is a key selling point. Most of the most recent cryptocurrencies are available right here. The trade volume on Gate.io is also impressive. It ranks among the top 20 most active stock exchanges in terms of trading volume almost every day. The daily trade volume is about $100 million. The most popular trading pairs on Gate.io often include USDT (Tether) as a component. This exchange's enormous number of trading pairs and outstanding liquidity, to recap, are two of its most striking features.

How To Store $UFO

Storage of UFO in hardware wallets is the last step.

Even though Binance is one of the safest cryptocurrency exchanges, there have been hacking events, stolen assets. If you intend to store your UFO for a long time, you may want to look at protecting it. Due to the nature of the exchange, wallets, which we refer to as "Hot Wallets," will constantly be online, exposing many risks. By far, the most secure method of keeping your coins is to use "Cold wallets," which only allow access to the blockchain (or simply "go online") when sending cash. This reduces the likelihood of a hacking event occurring. An offline-created combination of public and private addresses known as a "paper wallet" is a free cold wallet. You'll be able to write it down someplace and keep it safe. However, it is not a longterm solution and is vulnerable to various dangers.

Hardware wallets outclass cold wallets in this scenario. A USB-enabled gadget is frequently used to save your wallet's most crucial information in a more long-lasting manner. They have military-grade security built-in, and their software is updated regularly by the devices' makers, ensuring their continued safety. The most popular alternatives in this category are the Ledger Nano S and Ledger Nano X, which range in price from $50 to $100 depending on the capabilities they provide. In our view, these wallets are a wise purchase if you want to keep your money safe.

Is UFO A Good Investment?

Its market cap is still deemed tiny, which means that the price of UFO may be quite volatile when the market moves significantly, as it has increased by 949.67 percent over the previous three months. If UFO keeps growing steadily, it will likely see some significant increases shortly. The key to successful trading is never to lose sight of the big picture.

Remember that this is not financial advice.

Investors in cryptocurrency should do their due diligence and use extreme caution.

# Conclusion

The Metaverse remains a wholly new concept for technology and the rest of the world. Many regulators, innovators, and commerce merchants are rapidly in the race to understand and begin to ply their goods on the metaverse. While it is still very unclear where deliberations and disruptions of the metaverse might end, one thing is clear: the metaverse is here to stay.

The question to ask is: Are you willing to swim along with the tide?